CW00383167

ted
)orders

disrupted
borders

An intervention
in definitions
of boundaries

edited by **Sunil Gupta**

R
∿∿
O   RIVERS ORAM PRESS / LONDON

First published in 1993 by   Rivers Oram Press
144 Hemingford Road
London N1 1DE

Published in the USA by   Paul and Company
Post Office Box 422
Concord, MA 01742

Designed by   Eugenie Dodd Typographics
Electronic pre-press by   Michael Gibson
Set in   Janson and Meta
Printed in Great Britain by   John Goodman & Sons (Printers) Ltd
Birmingham

British Library Cataloguing in Publication Date
A catalogue record for this book is available from the British Library

ISBN 1 85489 044 1   (hardback)
ISBN 1 85489 045 X   (paperback)

Disrupted Borders is an OVA/INIVA initiative with a touring exhibition in collaboration with Arnolfini, Bristol and The Photographers' Gallery, London.

In memory of

Samena Rana
(1958 Lahore-1992 London)

Darrel Ellis
(1955 The Bronx-1992 Manhattan)

STRICKEN ON A JOURNEY,
MY DREAMS GO WANDERING ROUND
DESOLATE FIELDS.
Matsuo Bashô (1644-1694)

Contents

Sunil Gupta

Sunil Gupta is a London-based, Indian-born, Canadian citizen who works as a photographer, artist, curator and cultural activist.

Introduction

Disrupted Borders is my first curatorial project for INIVA[1] and is the basis for a contribution to its exhibitions programme. The idea behind this project lies in the interaction between the kind of specialised projects[2] I had been involved with in the last few years and the need to tie those ideas together. Since 1986 I have been involved in organising exhibitions around a variety of specialist themes to bring targeted audiences into the gallery. There have been lesbian and gay shows, Black and Asian shows, now I want to bring these issues not only into context with each other but also to confront the failure of modernism to take into account the wide variety of constituencies for the production and consumption of art on a world-wide scale. This Utopia, or 'new internationalism' of integration is assiduously attacked in all quarters of the globe. Are we replacing our modest achievements by tribalism? As the nation states of the nineteenth century give way to the regional superpowers of the late twentieth century the borders between them are getting ever more fortified.

Today we are witnessing a realignment of international and domestic politics. Culture is inevitably, intimately, woven into this fabric of change. A return to market economies is being heralded with a return to the aesthetic of artist as producer of commodity, despite the decline in the number of buyers. The rhetoric of devolved funding means that there is no adequate support for national and international strategic plans. It is into such a political climate that INIVA has been launched.

Disrupted Borders is also a story about journeys. The project is dedicated to two young artists who made their journeys in quite different parts of the world but found their subject matter equally bound by their

1 The Institute of New International Visual Arts was offered funding by the Arts Council of Great Britain from September 1993 to research the possibility of a new study and exhibition space for the UK

2 For example *An Economy of Signs: Contemporary Indian Photography, Ecstatic Antibodies: Resisting the AIDS Mythology*, both 1990

personal histories. Darrel Ellis moved from the Bronx in New York to Manhattan to become an artist and a black gay man. His work is an attempt to reclaim his biological family and the father he never knew. Samena Rana came to the UK from Pakistan for medical treatment as a teenager and found herself both in a wheelchair and without a voice. Her work is a testimony to her struggle to gain access to support and training as well as to bridge the gap between race, gender and culture.

In the 1980s in Britain, artists participated in a groundswell of demands that called for more equitable arts funding and a profiling of those practitioners who were not finding opportunities to develop their work because of a lack of commitment by the trustees of our cultural institutions. Simultaneously, Britain's international relationships were changing dramatically; from alignment with the Commonwealth to a bid for greater integration into the European community. The artists now face European institutions which have even less understanding of their needs.

The connecting threads in this book work across form and content. Starting with the very traditional genre of the photo-reportage story Shahidul Alam tells the important tale of a country achieving the vote for its citizens, a simple and crucial right not yet enjoyed by all peoples. Stuart Hall discusses the impact of the realignment of Europe both within and without its borders. Carol Condé and Karl Beveridge make complex visual works that reveal the erosion of working people's lives. Diane Neumaier shares her research on the shift in Russia as witnessed by its photographers. Stephen Dodd has written on the impact of modernity on the landscape of Japan as interpreted by its writers in the 1920s. Hagiwara Hiroko continues into the post-war era of Japan reviewing the work of a woman artist whose involvement with the plight of Koreans as an ethnic minority counters the high-tech image of that country currently being purveyed. Lisa Reihana writes about a programme of video tapes which reveals the extent and diversity of Maori cultural activism in New Zealand. Marian Pastor Roces writes about the tragic trade in human resources particularly involving Filipino workers in the Gulf States.

Jorma Puranen has made moving work that reclaims Sámi peoples' images from the vaults of the *Musée de l'Homme*, Paris and returns them 'home'. Clare Harris writes about the position of Tibetan artists trapped on the Indian side of the border trying to maintain cultural traditions bound up with isolation. Jamelie Hassan's piece is a recounting of another border crossing, that between the USA and Mexico. David Hirsh writes about the irony of Darrel Ellis's life that ended just before the Museum of Modern Art, New York was about to show his work. Sutapa Biswas was commissioned to extend her body of work around identity.

Timon Screech investigates the categorisation of human races and genders in Japan during the *Edo* period. Monika Baker uses the conventions of dressing up to explore gender in a commissioned piece. Sheba Chhachhi was commissioned to enable the construction of her new work around 'ecstatic' older women in India. Doug Ischar's work is about the representation of masculinity in relation to his father in 1950s America. Millie Wilson's piece is a work within her larger project, the creation of a 'Museum of Lesbian Dreams'. Samena Rana whose commission was cut short by her untimely death is represented by a completed piece and fragments of her last work in progress.

Emily Andersen and Renée Tobe were commissioned to make a new installation dealing with holistic medicine and its particular relationship to women. Claudine Brown and Deborah Willis-Braithwaite contribute an essay about their work in progress which is to set up a National African American Museum at the Smithsonian Institution, Washington. Helen Grace writes about the borders between different kinds of writing about art. Robert Atkins recounts the uplifting experience of a part of New York's art world responding to devastation by AIDS with commemorations to the artists' works that will never be made. In the same spirit, this book and exhibition is a commemoration to two young artists who were at the beginning of their careers and who never had an opportunity to meet. I think they would have had much to learn from each other.

I would like to thank all the artists and writers who appear in this book for their time and patience. Also, Barry Lane at the Arts Council for supporting this publication, Brett Rogers at the British Council, Clare Williamson and the Institute of Modern Art, Brisbane, Judith Mastai at the Vancouver Art Gallery, and Ian Rashid. Shaheen Merali at *Panchayat* and Allen Frame, New York for showing me the works of Samena Rana and Darrel Ellis. Tessa Jackson at the Arnolfini and Ruth Charity at the Photographers' Gallery who made the exhibition possible. My assistants Lana Wong, Sharmini Peirera, Jesse Kahn and Susan Banton who worked on all aspects of pre-production and administration. Sarah Wason whose efforts sustained the development of INIVA at the Arts Council. And finally Peter Cleary and Stephen Dodd whose kindness and trust have made this work possible.

Shahidul Alam

A Struggle for Democracy

Shahidul Alam is a self-taught photographer. Based in Bangladesh since 1984, he founded Drik Picture Library in 1989. Alam was the 1992 winner of the *Mother Jones Award*, a scholarship sponsored by Kodak and Apple Computers at the Centre for Creative Imaging, USA.

Alam's exhibitions include: *24 Hours in Guagzhou*, Nikon Gallery, London (1987); *When the Waters Came*, Side Gallery, Newcastle (1989); *Dhonu Mia*, an exhibition on the life of a rickshaw walla (on a UK tour since 1990); and several group exhibitions currently touring India, France, and Denmark. His published work has also appeared in the *New York Times*, *Los Angeles Times*, *Reader's Digest*, *Fifty Years of Oxfam*, and *After the Storm*.

1

This work was started on 10 November 1987 – Dhaka Siege Day. The people had united in a stand to overthrow the autocratic regime of General Ershad. A young worker, Nur Hossain, led one of the rallies. He had painted on his chest 'Let Democracy Live'. He was the first of many who were killed by the police in the movement. The sequence of events, over the backdrop of the everyday lives of people, is documented. The floods, opulent weddings, mourners at the martyr's memorial, military oppression on tribal groups in the hill tracts, rejoicing at Ershad's departure, and the election.

The second phase of this work includes events after the elections. The devastating cyclone on the 29 April 1991, and the reconstruction is the first part. The second part looks at attempts by the government to reinstate people who have committed crimes against the people for political expediency, the government's control of the media, corruption in the public sector and a series of interviews of politicians (including that of General Ershad), activists and others, as well as civil rights issues (Dhaka jail, Chittagong Hill Tracts, Rohingya refugees) and a look to the future.

▲ 10 November 1987, Dhaka
Siege Day. The commercial centre
of Motijheel is empty as
opposition parties unite to
oust a dictator

▲ There was direct confrontation
with the police. Bullets and
batons are countered by stones
from a thousand protesters. The
police later used machine guns

▲ Nur Hossain had written on his back 'Let Democracy Live' he was the first to die. A mural on a campus wall is painted in respect

▲ A biscuit-factory worker. There are no terms of employment and unions are illegal. The days he cannot work his family goes hungry

▶ A woman wades through the floodwaters in a street in Dhaka

▼ Surrounded by her worldly belongings, a woman cooks the family meal. The next day, the water had risen another three feet

▶ Not having eaten for three days, they wait in the rain for relief wheat, wondering if it will run out. Jinjira, flood 1988

▶ Guests at the wedding of the daughter of a powerful minister while the nation is still reeling from the effects of the floods

▲ Almost before the flood
waters have dried. The most
opulent wedding in our history

▶ A woman mourner at Shahid
Minar, the martyr's memorial, built
in memory of people killed by
government bullets

▶ A rickshaw puller's family live
in the factory; their home is a
4-feet square hut in the corner.
They earn about 6 rupees for
breaking 50 kgms of stone

▶ Once an agrarian family,
they are now forced into shrimp
cultivation by the big landowners.
There is no land left for grazing

▶ This once-fertile land is now a giant pond. 'Dollars swim in the water', say the landowners

▼ Political repression is accompanied by fanaticism. Militant groups have set up torture cells and have cut off people's hands

▶ 'All quiet on the hill tracts', the official version; the tranquillity of a tribal home

▶ Military presence in the hill tracts converted this serene landscape into a war zone. Sometimes entire villages are razed to the ground

▲ The night of 4 December 1990,
the dictator agrees to step down.
Jubilant people take to the streets

▶ For the first time in the history
of our nation, a fair and free
election. A stamp on a ballot
paper in exchange for Nur
Hossain's death

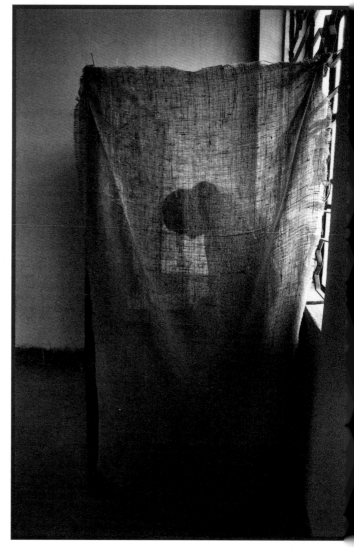

The People's Republic of Bangladesh

Dear Prime Minister,

As a citizen of a nation with a democratically elected parliament, I write with some concern my feelings regarding the appropriation of Bangladesh television by the government. A media which is paid for and rightfully belongs to the people.

After the fall of the Ershad regime one had expected to see a change in the traditional propaganda that had been passed as news. Last night's news was a blatant and sad reminder that nothing has changed.

What happened at Suhrwardy Uddayan on 26 March 1992, might not have been in the interests of the ruling party. There may be a debate over the validity of the trial, but it is surely impossible to deny that probably the largest public gathering since 1972 had taken place. For a democratically elected government it is shamefully hypocritical to deny that the people had made a statement.

The news last night mentioned the parade in the morning, a small march past in Ghazipur, violence in distant lands, even the man of the match in a game of cricket. Nowhere was there a reference to the fact that almost a million people had gathered that morning for a public trial of a war criminal.

At a time when we are trying past perpetrators for misappropriation of public funds making people accountable, stealing the voice of an entire nation is a crime beyond redemption. Whatever we may call what television is showing today, it is certainly not 'the whole truth'.

It is a trying time in our land. The problems are many and the resources slender. What we need most now is national unity. That can surely not be achieved by alienating people, by withdrawing trust.

I believe that it is a time for reconstruction, and that the new government must be given a chance. I believe it is a time to forget our differences and rally together to rebuild this land that so many have sacrificed for. For that to happen there must first be honesty, and a government of the people must never turn against the people. The government must establish its credibility. For people to believe, the truth must be spoken. Then only can there be a real dialogue.

For this nation to succeed we need a responsible government, a responsible opposition and a responsible citizen. Surely the government can lead by example.

This struggling nation expects a lot from its leader. It needs your strength, your courage, your sensitivity. Above all it needs your sincerity.

Do not disappoint us.
I wish you well.

Shahidul Alam

Bangladesh Zindabad.
27th March 1992

Stuart Hall   **Stuart Hall is Professor of Sociology at the Open University.**

The New Europe

Europe is unstable. The economic collapse and nationalist conflict in the East is one factor, but there also seems to be a general challenge to mainstream politics developing in the West. In Denmark we saw the first street-level challenge to EC government from Brussels and Strasbourg. Leaving aside the trouble in the East, what exactly do you think is occurring in the West? Is this challenge to mainstream politics just a short-lived malaise or does it result from more fundamental social and economic troubles which might prove of great long-term importance?   I'm not yet sure a general pattern can be identified in Western Europe, although there are some disturbing signs. The German problem is serious because, in relation to unification, they have taken on a bigger problem than they expected, which has thrown them off-course. That will not force a fundamental shift of direction, but it will limit Germany's role and, from a broad EC viewpoint, Germany had an obviously stabilising and leading role. This is not an entirely negative factor, because Germany's role was going to be very closely linked to the needs of the Bundesbank. But undoubtedly there are some very nasty counter tendencies developing in Germany.

However, Italy is much more worrying. The patched-up political structure is coming apart at the seams. The League's success in the North of Italy and the Fascist success in the South are both signs of dissatisfaction with the old structures but, with respect to the League, of a very ambiguous political kind. And France is unstable – Socialism is already in retreat, Mitterand is on the way out and serious regional racism is rising. So Europe is very unstable which is surprising, since we were supposed to be witnessing the triumph of unification.

The Danish situation does not seem to be simply a purely regressive anti-European reaction. The Danes appear to be resisting the forms of welfare-state provision which they saw emerging in the new Europe and these were very much the private insurance schemes that are prevalent in the German welfare state. The Left saw Europe in a positive light because it seemed that although unification was a capitalist vision

A version of this interview with Adam Lent was first published in *New Times* 27 June 1992

there were aspects of it which acknowledged partnership between the private economy and the state and was more open towards state intervention and regulation.

The other version of the European project was the rampantly free-market Major-Thatcher approach. What is uncertain is which version is winning out. The entry of the Scandinavian countries might have strengthened the social welfarist perspective but it seems that exactly those formations are breaking-up. Those coalitions around the left of Christian Democracy have always been closer to the social market than the market forces ideal, and it was always important that those forces were strengthened. But it is the former system that is being undermined by the popular reaction against the existing coalitions and alliances.

Finally some European experience does reveal problems that arise from moving to new electoral systems. They do not quite guarantee the expression of democracy and stability that they were supposed to.

So you do not feel it is possible to identify the forces that might pick up support from the breakdown of left, Christian Democrat consensus? No, it is not yet clear. If you think of the Socialist Parties. especially the Italian and French, they have all pioneered Thatcherite styles of modernisation. So it is unlikely to be them. And the new alliance around what was the Italian Communist Party does not have the vision or perspective which will enable it to provide a stable opposition.

The European perspective for Britain is still very positive but it is a question of which perspective and whether this new openness and uncertainty will allow a new kind of regrouping of a democratic, Socialist left in Europe with a vision of a more democratised EC, which would undoubtedly go slower on the economic front. After all, how could a Europe in which people could hardly speak each other's languages, or name each other's capitals, produce a unified political community the day after tomorrow?

We have been bemused by the Thatcherite attempt to gain benefits out of a common market without the social and cultural consequences. This was never on. The Left needs to have the confidence to support a European perspective and think more about a slower building up of democratic, political organisational forms and civil society and cross contacts which would create genuine common markets. You cannot have economics moving one way and politics and culture the other.

You seem to be saying that the Left's approach to Europe has to be one that involves their own distinct vision, unlike the Labour Party attitude which is really without vision. Absolutely. The Labour Party is in favour of a greater commitment to the social charter but they have not built much of a consensus around it.

If we could just expand on the need for greater vision from the Left on Europe to a general vision of society, do you feel that the basis for an intellectual-political renewal, rather than an immediate organisational-political renewal, is being built through the ideas that are now flowing from green ideals and principles of radical democracy? Or might they come from other sources? There are many areas in which useful thinking is going on. Even the disaster of the Rio summit will give a kick to ecological consciousness. Questions of constitutional reform were around during the 1992 General Election, albeit in a truncated form.

There are plenty of ideas but what is lacking is the climate in which those ideas become articulated to political projects. Part of the problem is that the Labour Party undertakes its thinking with a very restricted axis. They have a kind of tame, intellectual elite but they do not have any connection to and are deeply suspicious of, any wider intellectual currents. This is astonishing given the fact that not only academia but all intellectuals in Britain tend to have to make their living through teaching, and that education has been so badly treated by the right. Additionally many of these intellectuals are absolutely dying for somebody to talk to them but nobody does. In some areas there are not many ideas around on the central question of what is the nature of 'the public' under conditions where Socialism and radical reform are not going to be administered by a unified and coherent state power; how does the state relate to a much more diverse range of publics? It cannot be understood in terms of five-yearly elections or opinion polls. And the critical question about how we escape from the old bureaucratic, clientist forms whilst avoiding the Thatcherite model is not addressed either. Thinking and ideas are coming from those working in the public sector and are not tied to the old, centralised bureaucracies. But they are not part of a wider debate.

There is a wide range of activities underway. There are campaigns for Centre-Left realignment, for constitutional

*reform and there is a plethora of social movements which are
still active despite the attacks of the last thirteen years. How
can those movements begin to come together? Should they be
trying to get together?*

There are different strategies. One is to work out if there is some type of organisational form which might create better contact across different groups, but without electoral reform that formation could be cut to ribbons. You have to think carefully about how we might insert such a formation into the two-party system, both because there are constituencies that need change now and cannot wait for another decade and because a fifth Conservative term will finish us all off.

The more important concern is the Labour Party and its instrumentality and connection with a range of movements and ideas in civil society they do not need formal, organisational linkage but a radial point into the thinking and strategy of the Party. There are two ways to go. One is a kind of semi-autonomous, quasi-party organisation made up of those elements left out of the particular political configuration. This raises the question of how does that bring itself to bear on the actual electoral mobilisation, voting and tasks of forming a government. On the other hand, can we change the Labour Party so that it acts not as the agent of its own rather sclerotic thinking, but as the conduit for a much wider set of ideas, movements, agitations and experiences? It is unclear which option might be more successful. In some ways it might be easier for those groups to talk to one another because they have many political and cultural things in common. But that means you leave the Labour Party to wither on the vine, which would have very serious consequences for the balance of political forces.

*What then are the political and cultural things that these
various progressive forces have in common? For example the
Socialist Movement, has not been eminently successful.
Attempts to bring together different groups only seems to
highlight their differences.*

These groups are the consequence of a fragmentation of the political landscape which does not easily cohere into an overall vision of a future social direction. That is one problem. Another is that simply by networking the social movements and other currents as they stand is sufficient to bring them up against the actual trend and direction of society. That is the disciplining factor.

These things must have a purchase on a society which is not currently giving ecological questions the kind of priority they want and which is still deeply committed to an individualist path to success. Unless you do come into sharp conflict with these factors, the movements and currents are working in a slightly protected vacuum. They are talking to one another but they have to think about the world out there in which they are going to have to mobilise if they are going to have an impact on the majority.

And do you think that it is ideas around democracy and pluralism and citizenship that could bring these groups into coalition and begin to have an impact on the society they are trying to change? Those are critical questions. The language of rights is the only currently available one that has a lot of popular purchase and depth in which to articulate the needs of individuals and collectives. There are problems with the language of citizenship because it is very individualised – it does not assimilate easily to collective needs and collective demands.

A second issue is that needs themselves are diversified. Society has been pluralised by different experiences, aims and social worlds and the language of citizenship is pretty universal in its origins and its characteristic forms. To reflect a diversity of needs through a universalist language means there must be some negotiation which the groups involved in citizenship have not fully taken on. There is a tension between the universal rights that citizenship delivers to all, regardless of race, gender, etc., and the differentiated specificity of the needs which different groups have.

The overall political question is how to integrate those different specific needs within some common political project. How to link the aspirations of the rising social strata, who still see their fortunes linked to the breakaway of the private sector and privatisation, with the completely differentiated needs of a very large underclass who cannot command an electoral majority?

The rising strata may not be paid-up Thatcherites, but they can see that the good things that have happened to them in last ten years have somehow been brought about by the break-up of the social-democratic landscape. Citizenship might be able to provide some rights to the underclass but you have to appeal to those other social strata who might not be convinced that they will get anything good out of it.

*You have described Majorism as 'unhegemonic'. Do you
therefore think it will be easier for progressive forces to make
headway against the Conservatives over the next four or five
years? Maybe the election result has made you revise your
view that Majorism is in fact 'unhegemonic'?*
The figure of Major as a
political device was rather
successful in stitching together a movement towards a more altruistic, less
abrasive view than Thatcherism, with a little more attention to the social
fabric, and to the people who have been left out without actually making
people pay the cost. He is much nicer, and obviously not wanting to grind
the faces of the poor in the dust but he is not going to put a price on it either.
So it remains unsure whether or not it is hegemonic. And while Majorism
has no distinctive project of its own, it is still deeply attached to the
Thatcherite project.

This means the reconstruction of the institutional life of
society, which is still rolling along. Major gives his own gloss to that which
makes it slightly more acceptable to public opinion but it has not halted that
underlying drift. And people have not latched on to this. There is rather
more momentum in the Thatcherite project than we imagined.

In the echelons of liberal opinion the usual British pragma-
tism seems to be emerging and this will adapt quietly and eventually to
practically anything. If the government were to say 'let us murder half the
population because we have to deal with the population problem', of course
there would be outrage. But six months later, the liberal echelons would say
'well, we cannot do anything about it, it has been legislated for, we should
be thinking about how we can do it humanely'. The *Guardian* recently had
four articles saying that it was ridiculous to publish the league tables of
schools but, since we have to, we will find the best way of doing it. That kind
of pragmatic adaptation to anything that is put forward is well established.

The third time around the BMA will not resist the NHS
reforms in the same way; teachers are more demoralised than ever, higher
education is already being restructured and there has never been any substantial political force blocking that. In that sense we are still on the rolling
tide of the Thatcherisation of society and Major is still attached to that
underlying project.

On the other hand, if the Tories were transforming society
and delivering on the economic front, it would be very hard to see any
openings but the weakness of the economy just opens the gap within which
other doubts can be seeded.

*But what is terrifying is that Thatcherism and the
Conservative Party has this incredible ability to maintain the
kernel of faith in market forces whilst still sopping up and
adapting itself to the accusations of its opposition. For example,
on the green issue Major has adapted himself towards an
emphasis on consumer protection and the public interest. So,
even if that anger that you identify does come through, will
the groundswell ever be strong enough to overwhelm the*
Tories or will they once again be able to adapt to survive?

You are absolutely right, but it is impossible to answer in the abstract. We have underestimated the elan with which a party can be unscrupulous about opportunism and principles. Nevertheless many of the doubts we have identified are diametrically opposed to Tory philosophy, and they are sitting on top of a society without commanding even a normal electoral, popular majority. And they are aware of the fact that in order to remain in a hegemonic position they must constantly adapt, absorb, translate and transform. They are constantly buying in from society, whether it is ecology or consumer needs, and transforming ideas into their own language, by a bit of lying and bit of deception.

We cannot say if they will always be able to do that until the question is asked: is the left doing the same thing? And it is not. The left is not attentive to all sorts of ideas, movements, antagonisms and needs being formulated out there in society, which it has to bring into its own orbit, to transform into a wider programme and to begin to shape legislation. The left does not function in relation to society in the same way. If it did there would be two political forces that are trying to reflect civil society within the framework of their own legislative and political philosophies.

*You said that a fifth Conservative term would finish us all off,
so the inevitable question asked in semi-desperation, is what
can we do to stop that fifth term? You seem to place some of
your faith in the economy but obviously there is very little that
progressive forces can do now to affect that.*

Many local things can be done. Alternative visions do not arise only from committees. For example, if we put some resources into a campaign to stop the destruction of our education system. We could not do it simply around defence of the old comprehensive system, we would have to ask, 'How could we construct an education system that would actually work effectively for the disenfranchised majority and create an educated public?'

A lot of parents, including the so-called privatised, well-off middle-class sector, still have kids in the public education system and they would respond to such a discussion. Neither the Labour Party, or teachers' unions are sufficiently attentive to the genuine fears that different sections of society, such as women, blacks and middle-class parents have about the unsuccessful delivery of education as a mass public service. There is a huge range of people who would get involved in a debate on public education. Such a debate might oblige Labour and the unions to put some of their resources and political power into connecting with this public discussion and agitation.

You are suggesting that the left switch away from the defensive role it has been playing for so long now. That brings us back to the question of vision because vision is central to any hegemonic project and the objective of creating peoples' identities.

I am not opposed to the defensive role. Anyone who works in the public sector will know that half your day is going to be spent defending the base, so that there is something from which to build. But being locked into the defensive conception has been the ruin of the so-called attempts to renew the left.

It is a project that has started ten years too late, it should have started in 1983.

Yes. When we called for rethinking on the left, it was not for a cosmetic dropping of the parts that the polls tell us are not going down too well in Basildon.

The idea was to free the ideals from the forms – the existing forms were not generating and delivering the ideals. If you think that education should be much more widely accessible as a critical resource of post-industrial society, you should not fight to the death to defend the particular forms in which that ideal was institutionalised in the 1950s. Open yourself, on the basis of that ideal, to the critique of the old form and then ask yourself what strategies are there for re-embodying those ideals in forms which meet the more differentiated structure of the population and the new needs of knowledge and so on. That is the only way to construct a vision.

The Labour Party has been at the centre of much of what you have said. But the next two years are going to see major changes in the nature of the Labour Party. With the

exception of Prescott, all those running for leadership posts
have a European Social Democratic Party vision for Labour's
structure. This will obviously entail a split with the unions:
much has been said about the effect this might have on the
party, but what effect, do you feel, will it have on the unions? It
was interesting during the election that NALGO, a union not
affiliated to Labour, ran quite a strident campaign. Do you   Loosened from the formal-
think that a split with the Party might liberate the unions?   ised, bureaucratic organisational bonds, the unions might be liberated into a more effective role. But
then there will be a real problem about funding the Labour Party and it is
difficult to see an immediate way around that. But in the long term both elements would benefit by splitting. The Labour Party would have to face the
fact that in terms of individual membership commitment it is a dead organisation. The Labour Party is kept alive by building in massive blocs of support and the block vote is completely deadly to the formation of political
consciousness, as it always has been. It paralyses the political will, political
investment, and political identification and that is what the Labour Party
lacks. It is an electoral machine that exists without having to forge direct
lines into the interests and consciousness of its constituents. So, if one can
overcome the important issue of finance, both the Labour Party, in having
to forge a new democratic relationship to its members, and the unions, as
having to play in a more open political field in relation to other parties and
organisations, would find a split to be a very positive thing.

Carol Condé and Karl Beveridge

Interventions

Carol Condé and Karl Beveridge work collaboratively and live in Toronto. They have completed several projects with trade unions and community groups over the past fifteen years and helped found the *Mayworks Festival of Working People and the Arts* and the *Artist and the Workplace* program which funds artists to work in residence with trade unions. They are founding members of the *Independent Artists' Union* and members of *Canadian Artists' Representation*.

▶ *Shutdown,* 1991, handpainted billboard, Windsor, Ontario

Why would you want to do art about our experience. We're not important.

It's a comment we often hear from working people. It speaks volumes about the negative experience of working life in our society and what the dominant culture has done to peoples' perceptions of themselves. But it can also be seen as an expression of resistance. Not being important is important! Doing a job, living in a community, having fun are important. What's being resisted is the bread and butter of middle-class existence – competitive individualism. What's being valued is collective fulfilment. While it's clear that working-class experience is re-written and trivialised by corporate culture and that this has profound effects on working-class perception, it's far from a complete rout.

While there is resistance to competitive individualism, there's also an attraction. While workers often view professionals with suspicion, they also work hard to send their kids to college. It's a way out. Corporate media hacks and their poorer fine arts cousins constantly re-package the middle-class dream in working-class clothes. After a while it's hard to tell who's who.

We're skilled at what we do. You're skilled at what you do. Our contribution is the work we do. You make the art.

The problem of class voice is complicated by the divisions of manual and mental labour that underlie the production of culture.

▲ *Free Expression*,
75 x 100 cms,
cibachrome print,
1989

Manual 'drudgery' versus intellectual 'wit'. A social division of labour that's resented by working people and abused by most of us who work on the professional side of the tracks. A division that limits their ability to act culturally and our ability to create meaningfully. It sets the terms of our negotiations with union and community members and is the reason we work with community movements. As institutions they provide the means by which we can share common beliefs if not common experience and forms of knowledge. It's also based on trust. A trust that we do not abuse the social privileges afforded cultural work. A trust that personal and individual interests are balanced by collective interests.

It's not only important to articulate the concerns of working and community life, but the work should also be able to stand up to the sophistication of corporate culture and take into account the complexities of cultural representation. If not, the work remains outside of peoples' frame of reference. You end up talking to yourself and a few specialised friends. It's also necessary to argue for a community based practice in the arts and begin to articulate a class politic around the democratisation of access to cultural resources.

Free Expression (1989) and *Shutdown* (1991) are a response to the free-trade agreement signed between Canada and the US in 1988.

▲ *The Pursuit of Excellence, Part I*, 60 x 75 cms, cibachrome print, 1989-90

Under this agreement all trade barriers will be eliminated leading to the eventual economic integration of the two countries. There are clauses 'protecting' Canadian social and cultural institutions, so long as they don't interfere with trade. This means that the odd painting might be protected. The agreement is being currently extended to include Mexico. Eventually they hope to include all of the Americas. Under the new agreement the division of interests becomes clearer. Put bluntly the US will serve as the centre of management and capital, Canada a source of raw materials and Mexico a supplier of cheap labour. Under the existing agreement these intentions are already evident. Canada has lost over 400,000 manufacturing jobs in four years. Comparisons between the North American Free Trade Agreement and the EC are problematic. The relative power of the US in comparison to its 'partners' is overwhelming in itself. But the North American Free Trade Agreement does not incorporate a social charter or any social protections. It's purely economic: that is, it surrenders political power to corporate market forces.

      Free Expression was originally commissioned by *FUSE* (an alternative arts magazine published in Toronto). The image focuses on the publishing industry. Most Canadian magazines are heavily subsidised because of US competition and the 'spread' of the Canadian market. These

▲ *The Pursuit of*
Excellence, Part II,
60 x 75 cms,
cibachrome print,
1989

subsidies can be considered an unfair trade advantage under the terms of free trade. The concept behind the image itself is a reversal of the 'Radio Free Europe' advertisements sponsored by the US Information Service in the 1950s and 1960s. The Corporate KGB enforcing free market censorship.

    Shutdown was produced as part of a public art/billboard series commissioned by Artcite (an artists-run centre in Windsor, Ontario). Windsor is an auto town across the border from Detroit. It has been particularly hard hit by free trade. To function as a billboard the image is direct and simple. No ambiguity here. It seemed to hold its own next to a MacDonalds burgerboard – a harbinger of future employment.

    The billboard was hand painted from the original photograph. It was too costly to photographically reproduce one billboard.

The Pursuit of
Excellence (1989-90)

In 1988 police stopped a stolen car. The driver, Wade Lawson, was an unarmed black youth. Scared, he drove off. The cops shot him in the back. He was killed instantly. Four years later, the cops were acquitted of any wrongdoing. There have been several similar incidents in Canada involving people of colour and native people. As yet,

SHUT DOWN FREE TRADE

▲ *Shut Down Free Trade*, photograph for billboard, 1991

no cop has been convicted or disciplined. The press gives the impression that such incidents have only occurred in the recent past, but the history of Canada is founded on such racial violence.

In 1989, the black community in Toronto protested an exhibition at the Royal Ontario Museum. The exhibition featured nine-teenth-century African art 'collected' by Canadian military and missionary types. The protest eventually forced the resignation of the curator and a public apology from the museum. Of more importance, however, was the public discussion of the gentler side of racism. Cultural exclusion and appropriation. Many failed to see that quality has to be preceded by an 'E' and that cultural meaning is socially, not institutionally, determined.

A major concern informing the two images was the need to depict racism from the point of view of a white person – namely ourselves. We also wanted to depict racism without representing those who are oppressed by it. It's a white problem, not a problem of those who are its target.

Dealing with the issue of unemployment and poverty is difficult. There's little that's positive about poverty. Images depicting the negative side do little more than reproduce stereotypes. How

Our Poverty is Their Power (1992)

▶ *Our Poverty Is Their Power*
Poster (offset)
50 x 40 cms, 1992

do you represent the insanity of a corporate driven society that coldly relegates twenty-five per cent of the population to poverty, calls them lazy, and then shifts more money to the already wealthy?

The poster image was based on informal discussions with many unemployed and poor people. They were angry, not only with the situation they found themselves in, but with a society that's indifferent to their poverty: at corporations that lay off a thousand workers and then donate a few pounds of milk powder to a food bank; at both left and right-wing governments that cut basic social programmes in the name of deficit reduction; at the welfare system that's constructed to demean and demoralise the people that it claims to assist.

There's also a sense of humour. Last Spring, the Coalition Against Poverty organised a march into a wealthy Toronto neighbourhood. An uneasy alliance between the working and non-working. They deposited symbolic bags of money on the doorsteps of corporate criminals. Steal from the poor and give to the rich.

The poster was produced as an Artists and the Workplace project in collaboration with the Ontario Coalition Against Poverty and the Labour Council of Metro Toronto. Artists and the Workplace is jointly funded by the Ontario Arts Council and the trade union movement.

Diane Neumaier

Diane Neumaier lives in New York and is a photographer and writer at Rutgers University, New Jersey. Her humorous feminist critiques of the museum system include the exhibitions *Metropolitan Tits*, *Metropolitan Dicks*, and *Museum Studies*, and the artist books *Building the Museum* and *Made to Shop*. She is the editor of the forthcoming anthology *ReFramings: New American Feminist Photographies*, and the co-editor of *Cultures in Contention*. Neumaier is the organiser of *Photo/Foto*, a series of Russian-American exchange exhibitions, residencies and symposia. She has worked at the Brooklyn Museum, served as a Museum Educator, Manager of School and Youth Programs and as Assistant Director of Government and Community Relations. She has contributed articles to *Patterns in Practice*, *Selections from the Journal of Museum Education* and *Something for Everyone*, *Access to Museums*.

Re-Representing Russia

Just as any situation in Russia begins to make sense, contradictions become evident and common sense must yet again be suspended. And now that I have cultivated the willingness to abandon previous understanding of 'the Russian Way' – it becomes almost impossible for me not to contradict anything I myself say about contemporary Russian culture.

Thus, writing these reflections has become a kind of riddle. Each time I return to the computer I find I don't know how to re-enter my own narrative or critique of what I have experienced since summer 1991 through three trips to Russia and all my subsequent contact with Russians here in the US. It is essential to note that I experience Russia, as an American, an American eager to cross over into an unfamiliar experience long forbidden by the Cold War. And, I must further identify myself as part of a Western international intellectual art community that understands images not simply as a reflections of social and political circumstance, but a fundamental political force. These ideas, basic to my own orientation, are completely foreign in Russia. What follows is a response to sharing much tea and vodka, and the viewing and discussion of many, many photographs.

In June 1991, as a representative of the Rutgers Center for
Innovative Printmaking in their five-year exchange programme with the
Soviet Union of Artists, I was the guest of the Union at their lakeside printmaking facility, Senej House of Art, near Moscow. Being a photographer
rather than a printmaker cast a shadow of doubt upon my worth as an artist,
yet I was generously provided an interpreter and an allowance and was set
loose in Moscow. Bearing a letter introducing me to the newly formed
Russian Union of Art Photographers, I made my way down crumbling
steps to the Union's damp basement darkroom, office and meeting rooms.
I have been working with this Union ever since on a constellation of photographer, exhibition and symposium exchanges; but I still cannot quite
explain how I have allowed the 'Russian Way' to restructure
my life.

My investigation has occasioned me to see nearly one-hundred portfolios of contemporary Russian art photographs.
I have chosen work which may give clues as to how some
contemporary Russian photographers and artists are
influenced by increased exposure to the West, how they
absorb or resist so-called post-modern practices, and especially how they think about visual culture today.

Since the 1930s the Soviet Union of Artists, as well as the
local and republic-level official artists' Union, have played
major roles in both facilitating and policing Soviet art production. While Union policies are correctly understood as
having effected repression and censorship, it must also be
noted that the Unions, had conscientiously considered
artists' material needs by providing studio space, stipends,

▲ Sergei Gitman, *Park and
Wasteland*, 1981, black-
and-white photograph

retreats, exhibition space, etc. The unions' recent loss of funding is among
many political and economic factors that have eroded their power and
many members' working and living conditions.

More than half a century of so-called 'official' art, accompanied during the last few decades by an 'unofficial' underground art, is
currently undergoing radical transformation. What was politically 'hot' in
the late Soviet Union has become commercially 'hot' in the West. Western
art dealers are having a field day

The Russian Union of Art Photographers, formed without
government support during the last year of the Soviet Union, is a hybrid of
the old, Soviet-style artists' unions and new, Western-style arts institutions

▲ Alexander Agafonov,
Amongst Symbols-V,
1992, hand-coloured,
black-and-white
photograph

which have cropped up in Moscow since the advent of Perestroika such as
the Institute for Contemporary Art and the Center for Modern Art. These
rapidly developing organisations have established strong relationships
with the West that affect the distribution as well as the character of contemporary Russian art.

In Russia, self-identified 'fine art photographers' are often
isolated, or isolate themselves, from other visual artists who find it of interest to employ or address photography. The Russian art-photography community and the Russian art world alike may be influenced more directly by
their counterparts in the West than they are by each other. One might even
argue that there is a strident refusal of interest in each other by those who
identify primarily as photographers or as artists; but it is important to
recognise that documentary and conceptual uses of photography are
merely different methods or strategies of image making, not necessarily
methods in conflict with each other. Towards this end I do not always make
a distinction here between these mutually exclusive categories.

Many Russian photographers and artists re-present already existing visual material, especially mass-produced and popular imagery. The vast majority of Russian artists who consciously or unconsciously appropriate or recycle images certainly do not maintain a self-conscious post-modern identity. Russian re-representations (that is, pictures of pictures) often look more up-to-date in a Western sense than any other Russian art photography style; but rather than positing critique of representation, these images function conceptually, or as documentary reports on the social life of pictures in Russia. Soviet artists' experiences of being driven by principles and manifestos was displaced politically by a less theoretically oriented art.

Moscovites Sergei Gitman and Alexander Agafonov (officials of the Russian Union of Art Photographers) are aware of the presence, as well as the absence, of other images within the photographic frame. Their works embody an irony which is very Russian. Sergei speaks metaphorically about Soviet society in an early 1980s photograph, while in 1991 Sascha Agafonov seized an opportunity to make a joke about Perestroika when a street photographer demanded that the Union store his tourist props during a rainstorm. The sarcasm these photographers employ is typical of late-Soviet humour about a system they find doesn't work. While their work occasionally addresses institutional failures, through their union work they attempt themselves to reinvent such structures. Thus both bear double, burdens of producing their own and facilitating others.

A pioneer of post-Soviet conceptual photography, Boris Mikhailov of Kharkov, Ukraine has for over twenty-five years incorporated a wide range of photographs and other visual images within his many varied series. Although he is not a Russian he is internationally acknowledged to be the father of Russian conceptual photography. Mikhailov's practice of image appropriation was the earliest Soviet photographic signal that visual imagery itself is a fundamental social element and that it is subject to visual analysis. Through his reworking of found and self-generated images – including snapshots, pornography, self-portraiture, documents of everyday life and records of Soviet celebrations – Mikhailov subverts ordinary meanings.

Boris's destabilising manipulations such as garish hand-colouring and disruptive hand-writing on prints, surreptitiously ridicule Soviet power while sympathetically representing Soviet people. To many

Westerners these interventions may seem unruly or naive, but to his local audiences they bring on gales of laughter and exclamations of recognition. Within his own culture Mikhailov's works are clear, efficient and concise. His razor-sharp *Sots Arts* projects which precisely undercut Soviet authority have provoked long explanations from my Russian friends about the subtleties of Soviet and post-Soviet life. After laughing nearly uncontrollably one young man began to shudder and confided to my how scary it was for him to remember and to criticise.

The range of Mikhailov's work is so wide that when I first viewed *The Missing Picture: Alternative Contemporary Photography from the Soviet Union* (an exhibition organised by John P. Jacob for the Massachusetts Institute of Technology [MIT] List Center), which featured Mikhailov's work and its relation to four younger Russian conceptual photographers, I found it hard to imagine that only one artist had produced such an immense range of work. In fact, when the show travelled to Lehman College in New York, at one point the gallery directors and I wrongly assumed that *Berdyansk – At the Beach*, an extensive project lov-

▼ Boris Mikhailov, from *Sots Art* series, 1975-90, hand-coloured, black-and-white photograph

ingly shot by Mikhailov in his own community was simply so straightfor-
ward that it must have been appropriated from another, less conceptually
oriented photographer, *Luriky* is a collection of his neighbours' personal
photos which Mikhailov playfully coloured by hand. The most voluminous
of his works are hand-made books; *Crimea Snobbery* address through his
own pictures and writing a whole constellation of social, psychological and
aesthetic issues. His recent panoramic views of Kharkov, stressing the
difficulties of daily life seem to have been produced by yet another author.
Mikhailov's portraits of his own family invite a Western psychoanalytic
reading of family dynamics that are surpassing. The astounding breadth
and depth of Boris Mikhailov's work underlies its varied influence on
younger artists.

▲ Galina Moskaleva,
Reminisence of Childhood,
1992, toned, black-and-
white photograph

Galina Moskaleva, like other Minsk,
Belarus artists, maintains regular contact
with Moscow art circles. Lithuanian born,
her new Belarussian 'nationality' is inconse-
quential to Russians; she was one of five
honoured photographers selected by the
Russian Union of Art Photographers to
represent them in 1992 and again in 1993.
Galina hand colours and tones black-and-
white photographs in a manner that was
once experimental but is now typical of
Minsk and of St Petersburg photographers.
Through memories of childhood produced by the snapshots that are the
foundation of her art, she explores how memory is experienced individu-
ally while it is produced socially. Galina is interested in the psychological
character of particular memories inspired by specific photographs rather
than the ideological role of vernacular photographic imagery. Her works
celebrate rather than analyse a personal past.

What makes Moskaleva's work significant to her home
audience is the way in which her personal memories re-stimulate their's.
Galina's work, reveals the way in which seemingly personal individual
experience is actually not so unique. In fact, even Galina's own past is not
really her own but one that had been presented to her intact: the courtship
of her parents. She juxtaposes the images of her young parents to period
movie posters; memory itself has disappeared, and something else, almost
nostalgically, stands in its place. Ultimately the effect of Moskaleva's use of

pictures is to rewrite, not to remember, the past. Most powerful of her
works are the pictures of herself as a little girl, often naked. Her adult effort
to look at her younger self is her means of writing herself. Whereas Boris
Mikhailov's family views reproduce unconscious desire, Galina
Moskaleva's exemplify self-conscious invention. Mikhailov deconstructs
the family; Moskaleva reconstructs it.

   Valery Shchekoldin is a prize-winning photo-journalist.
Like, Galina Moskaleva, he was selected as a 1993 honoured photographer
by the Russian Union of Art Photographers which shows the diversity of
the Union's membership. Just as deliberately as Moskaleva looks inward,
Shchekoldin looks outward. Like Mikhailov's documentation of his community, Shchekoldin's photographs are sympathetic to his subjects,
although cooler than the former's affectionate engagement. Valery's
Second World War Veterans series bears witness to the significance of
commemorative pictures within Soviet culture.

   Adopting conventional documentary means were familiar
long before Perestroika, Shchekoldin's practice seizes freedoms facilitated
by Perestroika, and targets what was forbidden including prisoners and the
military. (Another previously forbidden subject which Shchekoldin doesn't

▲ Igor Moukhin, *Untitled*,
1991, collage

pursue has been obsessively and oppressively focused upon by other art photographers: naked women – a sexist theme to which, please appreciate, I am not exposing you here! Pictures of naked women are understood as a sign of democracy, an expression of the demise of Communism and the former Soviet Union. I believe we will continue to see capitalism negotiated in post-Soviet culture at the expense of women, whose bodies already must be thinner and younger than before to be considered attractive.)

Shchekoldin's photographs reveal many aspects of Soviet and post-Soviet society. His method is in itself not innovative, the depth and range of his exploration of social categories is greater than that of any other body of work I saw in Russia. He is a compulsive photographer. He is always working – usually without adequate materials, always without decent facilities. At practically a moment's notice Valery gathered for me almost a hundred examples of his documentation of public monuments when, with the aid of a Russian-English dictionary, I told him of my interest in images of images. For Valery this theme is not a project, it is simply one of many ongoing themes about Soviet and post-Soviet daily life.

(We Westerners, who are committed to investigating issues of representation, find pictures of Soviet signs such as those by

Shchekoldin irresistible. Since the advent of the Cold War such images have also been employed in the west as anti-communist propaganda, proof of the totalitarian nature of communism. But it is my sense that in Russia, photographs like Shchekoldin's are understood as a more limited and literal record of a particular historical moment. The theoretical underpinnings of a critical politics of representation weren't at issue in any of the art photography circles with which I made contact. My critical orientation couldn't even spark discussion. However, within certain *avant garde* reaches of the art world, the interest in theoretical enquiry is strong. These worlds – the art-photography community and the art scene – hardly know each other and seem to like it that way.)

Igor Moukhin is a young artist who uses photography but deliberately does not associate with the Russian Union of Art Photographers although he maintains friendships with some Union photographers. Like Boris Mikhailov, Moukhin works in series each with their own theme and format. Like Mikhailov, some of Moukhin's series are comprised exclusively of found images; most feature a contest between systems of representation. Moukhin has also been working for years building an archive of his own photographs and historical materials that he will use in the future to document the placement, displacement and replacement of Soviet and Russian monuments. Igor has shown me his collections of commemorative pictures of particular monument sites over many years in which the monuments have been exchanged to suit the political moment.

Moukhin's photographs look more like Lee Friedlander's monuments (which are familiar to Moukhin) than they look like Valery Shchekoldin's monuments. Unlike Shchekoldin whose prolific documentation is left to editors to arrange, Moukhin's conceptual arrangements of his own pictures is an essential element of his work. Through dozens of images, Igor's ongoing Kremlin project discloses the material reality of the Kremlin, removing it from its representational ideological photo-masquerade. Igor shows us the Kremlin lurking behind street construction, behind garbage, behind all kinds of contemporary urban reality that is meant to be ignored, edited out of nationalistic architectural views. In one of his series he juxtaposes found images of Soviet workers within the frame of a Russian fine art convention from which these workers can only be alienated. Together Moukhin's photographs argue that politics is inseparable from representation. Embedded in Moukhin's work is the promise of a serious investigation of how meaning is made.

Gennady Goushchin, through his extraordinary collage, offers the most sophisticated and deliberate critique of representation I was exposed to in Russia. The day before I first flew to Moscow in 1991, I saw his work in an installation of *Photomanifesto* mounted Russian-style in a Baltimore bus terminal by The Museum for Contemporary Art. Overall, it reminded me of early 1970s art photography here in the US; the images by Goushchin were very different.

It was not easy to find Goushchin in Moscow. I learned that he is officially known as an abstract sculptor and painter, and was a long-standing member of the establishment Russian Union of Artists. He had been producing collage underground for more than twenty years, and only

▲ Gennady Goushchin,
Untitled, 1991, collage

recently was able to openly display these works. Once we did connect, after some detective work on my part and a good bit of luck, we ran into severe difficulty communicating, because each of the three interpreters we depended upon were unwilling to translate literally between us. Their own misunderstanding of Gennady's work simply made it impossible for them to listen. We tried simpler and simpler statements, and finally resorted to pointing to words in a Russian-English dictionary – which actually was an improvement. Eventually Gennady a cousin of his wife who teaches English at MGU, Moscow State University, came to our rescue.

What followed in the coming weeks were days of exchange, hours and hours of taped discussion about approximately forty collages through which Gennady gave me an introductory history of pre-Revolutionary Russian art and culture to accompany my scanty knowledge of Soviet art, enabling me at least to confirm the high level of critique I had sensed his collage offers. While some are accessible to an ordinary Western audience, most offer insights that we simply cannot understand. As with Boris Mikhailov's work, local audiences roar with laughter at first sight and then take the opportunity to explain to me intricacies of Soviet and Russian society.

Goushchin's work not only criticises propaganda under Soviet society, it discloses the social role played by Russian visual and literary culture long before the Soviet period and 'socialist realism'. An analysis of how meaning is produced and deployed is at the heart of his work. By associating, though not equating, those iconic cultural deities Pushkin and

Lenin through his collage, Goushchin complicates both. When the Soviet Union was still the Soviet Union, Gennady presented Mikhail Gorbachev as the conduit of transformation. The West, as personified by the Mona Lisa, peers through Gorbachev.

Alexei Shulgin's conceptual works force his viewers' attention to the constructedness of visual culture Shulgin is well-known for *Others' Photographs* his ground-breaking appropriation of an industrial archive of negatives he found and subsequently printed and re-presented as art objects. It is fascinating how difficult yet engaging it is to interpret the resulting work. The viewer is at once seduced into a formalist reading of how the ugly industrial images, by a simple shift of context, become beautiful. At the same time the viewer must account for the nature of the shift itself. Understanding how meaning is made is indeed an uncomfortable burden.

When I first saw these works shown along with those by three other young Moscow conceptual photographers in *The Missing Picture* exhibition, I was somewhat resistant to their 'high art look' the absolutely magnetic quality of Boris Mikhailov's work. However, as I have grown to know Shulgin's work within its Russian context, its seriousness and humour have won me over. While Shulgin is directly affected by Western conceptual art practices, he retools these art-world tendencies to address contemporary Russian problems. More than other artists, Shulgin demands his viewers work at looking.

Through a combination of photographic and sculptural means Shulgin emphasises the material nature of image and ideology. His *TV Set* series, which has been extensively exhibited in the US and Europe, incorporates actual TV front panels within which Shulgin frames what look like low-grade (Russian?!) reception colour television test patterns. These funny, sad images force the viewer to consider the media system with its liberatory possibilities and disappointing reality. We have before us something whose potential is to communicate and whose reality we cannot see. Like mass media everywhere and particularly like mass media in Russia, Shulgin simultaneously deprives and provokes us. Each of his television panels presents a unique, interchangeable, equally meaningless pattern. Shulgin does not make it easy for us; meaning is left to the devices of the viewer.

▲ Alexei Shulgin, from *Rotating Landscapes* series, 1992, photo-sculpture

«Я киноглаз. Я глаз механический. Я. машина, показываю вам мир таким, каким только я его смогу увидеть. Я освобождаю себя сегодня навсегда от неподвижности человеческой, я в непрерывном движении, я приближаюсь и удаляюсь от предметов. я подлезаю под них. я влезаю на них, я двигаюсь рядом с мордой бегущей лошади. я врезаюсь на полном ходу в толпу, я бегу перед бегущими солдатами. я опрокидываюсь на спину, я под–нимаюсь вместе с аэропланами. я падаю и взлетаю вместе с падающими и взлетающими телами»(Дзига Вертов).

▲ Catalogue spread from
Replica, Gallery Skola,
1991, quote and film
stills by Dziga Vertov,
photograph by Alexander
Rodchenko

'I am the eye of the camera. I am a mechanical eye. I am a machine and I show you the world as only I see it. Today I am freeing myself forever from human immobility, I am in perpetual motion, I move up to objects and then away from them, I crawl under them and onto them, I move alongside the muzzle of a galloping horse, I run at full speed into a crowd, I run in front of running soldiers, I collapse onto my back, I take off with aeroplanes, I rise and fall with rising and falling bodies'.

Likewise, Alexei's subsequent project, *Rotating Landscapes* is both hilarious and challenging. Shulgin has produced several variants in which traditional museum-style frames display generic-looking landscapes mounted on electrically powered, rotating devices. Naturally it is impossible to focus on the pictures. Again we are deprived, again we are provoked. It is only because this work is so goofy that the audience doesn't feel insulted by the assault. That Shulgin holds the media and the landscape image similarly accountable for blinding its public is a useful insight into how 'official' culture operates. Like Gennady Goushchin, through a dual treatment of media and landscape Alexei Shulgin associates the ideology of pre-Soviet and post-Soviet visual culture.

In 1991 Irina Piganova was encouraged to open Gallery Skola, the first Russian art photography gallery, which is strategically housed in the Moscow Center for Modern Art. While Piganova is not an artist herself, her interventions as a curator are so transformative that she could be considered a collaborator. And, when she collaborates with history – as she did with the works of Alexander Rodchenko and Dziga Vertov in Gallery Skola's premier exhibition, so as not to privilege any one contemporary artist with being exhibited first – we in the West could easily view the results as installation art. Gallery Skola's projects, like most institutional presentations, bring authorship itself into question. The first Gallery Skola collaborative catalogue, *Replica*, features degraded historical replications of the revered Rodchenko and Vertov and the text of the contemporary Russian critic and curator Tatiana Salzirn. Through the curatorial and critical interventions crossing over from conventional presentation as criticism to presentation as artwork, issues of display and representation are addressed by *Replica*.

While Piganova unabashedly assumes a Western, market approach to the display and distribution of art, she also assumes an American non-profit model for institutionally encouraging experimentation. For her, these are aesthetic as well as pragmatic innovations in response to a crumbling economy. Like most exciting Russian art practices, everything about Gallery Skola is a clever way of making do. When I first visited the space in 1991 I commented on the innovative use of display materials; to which Irina replied that there simply had been no white mount board in Moscow at the time the show had been installed. In some ways the principles Piganova embraces seem conversely related to those expressed in Revolutionary Russian constructivist manifestos.

▶ Diane Neumaier, *New World Order*, 1993,
colour photomontage

It is obvious that Russian artists are wrestling with their Soviet history. Yet the post-Soviet abandonment of socialist values in exchange for a Western-style consumer art marketplace is not as totalising as we in the West are led to believe. While socialist principles are attached to a totalitarian political history they are also attached to a Utopian imagination and to activist manifestos. Capitalism cannot substitute in post-Soviet culture for Revolutionary ideals. In the Western media the dual contests between socialism and capitalism and between totalitarianism and democracy have been ideologically conflated into a single struggle. Nonetheless, the economic and democratic protections that can be afforded by socialism, as well as the authoritarian potential of Russian governance that long preceded the 1917 October Revolution, remain ideologically embedded in post-Soviet culture.

Disappointed in their current government, with the so-called market, and among other things with Russian artists' experiences in the West, capitalism's reputation in Russia is not exactly flourishing. Recently I attended a symposium in the US on 'unofficial' Russian art and was given a good laugh by several unknown young Russian artists who, like me, having not been invited to the private aromatic dinner to which only our noses were treated, explained to me that America is just like home: instead of being excluded by the Soviet Union of Artists, they are now excluded by democratic American museums!

Thanks to Virginia Rutledge for patiently reading and discussing an early draft of this essay, to Viktor Lugansky for leading me to some of the works and for reproducing them for me and to Sergei Gitman for making my work in Russia possible

Stephen Dodd

The Railway as Rupture

The Writings of Shimazaki Tôson

Shimazaki Tôson, 1872-1943 was born in the countryside, spent his formative years in Tokyo and then devoted much of his adult literary career nostalgically evoking the lost ties to the countryside of his early childhood.

Stephen Dodd received his BA from Keble College, Oxford, and his PhD in 1993 in Modern Japanese Literature at Columbia University, New York. He taught at the University of California, Santa Barbara, before going to Duke University, North Carolina, where he is Assistant Professor of Japanese Literature.

The introduction of Western modes of thought into Japan from the beginning of the Meiji period (1868-1912) altered literary perceptions of the countryside in the writings of three late Meiji and Taishô writers; Shimazaki Tôson, Satô Haruo and Shiga Naoya. What exactly 'countryside' might signify is ambiguous. The English word 'countryside' describes something for which there is no exact equivalent in Japanese. The type of rural area which Satô Haruo seems most interested to depict, for instance, is what is called *den'en* in Japanese, a term which may best be translated into English as something like 'pastoral space'. The *den'en* is usually to be found just beyond concentrations of population, and is an area of land which has been physically worked as an agricultural area time after time.

Shiga Naoya, on the other hand, writes of a 'countryside' closer to the Japanese term, *chihô*, that is, the provinces. In his major novel, *A Dark Night's Passing*, the hero takes a trip to Mt Daisen, in Tottori Prefecture on the coast of the Japan Sea. This is a type of countryside very different from the sheltered area on the outskirts of a city, and was well-known as a place where religious mountain austerities had been traditionally practiced.

In Shimazaki Tosôn's writings, the countryside is more or less synonymous with the *furusato*, the home town or native place, that is, the place from which one originates and which often carries strong emotional overtones of where one's heart is.

For some, the countryside stood as a place of poverty and

ignorance and was hardly worthy even of consideration. For others, it was a symbol of purity, of essential Japanese-ness. The writer Yokoi Tokiyoshi, for example, compared the countryside favourably with what he saw as the corrupting influence of the city. But any discussion of the countryside must also include some consideration of an evolving city-centred consciousness.

The naturalist writer Tayama Katai has spoken of how, from the beginning of Meiji, Tokyo was gradually being built up as the capital of a 'new Japanese Empire'. Roads were widened, bridges rebuilt, and the water supply improved through the laying of pipes. The Tokugawa city of Edo was transformed into Tokyo by a physical reconstruction, but just as importantly by the release of a new set of aspirations and needs unleashed by the social changes of the age. Beginning with the construction of the Ginza shopping district with its brick buildings in the 1870s, Tokyo's new role was partly to serve as a show-case for Western fashions and innovations. The term *miyako* – referring to a traditional culture in the style of the older capital of Kyôto – did not fit the new city. Instead, it was given the title of *teito* (imperial capital), to signify the emerging nation straining to take its place among other so-called 'advanced' nations of the West in which aggressive imperial designs seemed an indispensable element.

A clear sign of the new economic potential of the Meiji capital was the shift away from a dependency on the waterways, especially around the important Shitamachi (or, downtown) area of Edo, to the development what has been called a 'land metropolis' (*riku no tô*). During the Edo period great bustling open spaces and celebrated sights alongside the water drew crowds of people, and many theatres even in the early part of Meiji were set up on the waterside.

However, the city's vigour was inevitably transferred from the low-lying Shitamachi to newly thriving areas. Edo inhabitants lamented that the culture of the Low City was dispersed as the rich moved away, and their patronage of the local arts was withdrawn. But though this break-up of the old city was sad for some, it led to the birth of a new one: Tokyo, a place which offered others a host of novel and exciting possibilities. Patronage from the rich gave way to a form of 'patronage' more in keeping with an emerging capitalist economy and publishing houses arose to satisfy a growing demand for the written word as literacy among the general population increased. One of the major groups of writers who emerged to meet that demand were those like Shimazaki Tôson who had moved to

Tokyo from their original homes in the countryside.

A sense of the confusion and excitement of a country boy's first visit to the big city with its masses of people is provided by Yamamura Icho in his short piece entitled *After Coming to the Capital* (Jôkyô-go, 1911). After his first ever railway ride, he arrives with his elder brother in Ueno Station:

'Ueno! Ueno!'
The platform attendant's voice was lost in a confusion of noises. I drew up to my elder brother and as we walked we were swept along on human waves. The clatter of clogs, cries of every kind, the train whistles and beams of light that stuck our eyes – bewildered by all these things, I was terrified I might have set foot in Hell.[1]

The boy would have been familiar in the countryside with the sound of clogs and with the occasional cry of merchants; but in the city, the sheer quantity of those sounds has made them a 'confusion of noises'. This is not the world he left behind; it embodies all that is fearful and unknown – a hellish place.

This inability to fully comprehend what Raymond Williams has called the 'crowded strangeness' of urban life is emphasised further when the two take a rickshaw to the house of an uncle where they will be staying:

We went right along the dark, almost deserted Yamashita road, and went over a railway crossing. Then we passed through a roadside district with its numerous, low-set houses where people did side-jobs in the gloomy lamplight, and with its shops selling sundries; then on past another street built up on only one side with a ditch smelling of mud set up in front, until we suddenly came to a place where dawn seemed to have broken.[2]

For the provincial naturalist, Tokyo appears as the source of everything that is new in Meiji Japan, from electric lights to ideas. It offered, too, a far more fluid set of possibilities. We can get some idea of this transformative effect of the city on its inhabitants by looking at Tôson's 1919 novel, *When the Cherries Blossom (Sakura no mi no juku suru made)*. He tells the story of a young man, Kishimoto Sutekichi, who is attending a Christian college in Tokyo. (As is often the case in his writings, it is based on the writer's own experiences: he studied at Meiji Gakuin, a Tokyo Presbyterian school, from 1887-91.) Kishimoto is visited by his mother from the countryside. After she leaves, he feels sad and takes a stroll around the city's bridges:

1 *Mita bungaku*, June 1911, vol.2, no.6, Kyôto Rinsen shoten, 1970-71, reprint, p.137

2 Ibid., p. 138

An unusual feeling welled up in Sutekichi's heart. He recalled vividly the childlike expectation he had felt the day he came from his distant home town to pursue his studies in Tokyo, the first time in his life when he saw a great city. It was the day when the horse coach they had taken along the Nakasendô highway stopped at the side of the Mansei bridge; when ... he and another youth ... stepped down together.... And he saw clearly the scene of the music halls and inns close to the avenue of trees where the carriage had stopped at Hirokôji.[3]

Now Tôson arrived in 1881. He describes his arrival as something which took place years ago. Both passages offer a child's first encounter with an urban landscape, but what was once the unknown to Sutekichi has become the stuff of a familiar and recoverable memory. Not only has a simple dichotomy between the unthreatening countryside and the fearful city been obliterated: experiences of the city now constitute an important part of what he is.

It is an uncomfortable awareness of this double aspect of his past by which he is now tied to both city and countryside, stirred up by his country mother's visit to the city, which disturbs him. After recalling these memories, Sutekichi 'felt like taking a walk through the streets in which he was brought up long ago'. His mother's departure leads him to seek solace in those Tokyo streets where his second family – corresponding to the Yoshimuras in real life – had raised him. His sense of belonging is tenuous, painful even, because it is also a sign of his separation from the original rural home.

The ambiguity with which Tôson depicts the city is also there when we turn to his writings about the countryside. Like that child travelling along the Yamashita road, there are limits to how far this writer, who has now returned from the city to his native place as a teacher, can fully know the environment he explores. For, if he is to attempt to reconcile himself with the countryside of his earliest years he cannot ignore his experience of city life. It is not possible for this writer to simply re-live the native place as if those intervening years had not left their mark. Having become a new type of city person, Tôson must re-experience the countryside with a new vision.

The power of Tokyo to attract people from surrounding areas was part of a general trend towards centralisation. Tetsuo Najita describes how:

himazaki Tôson, *Tôson shû* Chikuma shobô, 6-71, vol. 5, p.503

From the centre, comprehensive structures extended outward and downward to all parts of the nation. National geographical spaces had been redrawn with new systematic grids, administrative, political, industrial, and educational structures that overlapped each other.[4]

One of these new 'systematic grids' was the railway system. As an indication that Tokyo had become the centre of a new economic order, its main railway station, completed in 1914, appears in maps of the time as 'Central Station' (*chûô teishajô*), and this name signified not only the centre of Tokyo, but of Japan. The very descriptions of incoming and outgoing railway journeys in relation to Tokyo were inscribed with a new hierarchical system of authority. Kyôto and its environs had long been known by the alternative term of Kamigata, meaning the 'upper region', a reference to the elevated position of the Emperor who had lived there until the move to Tokyo at the beginning of Meiji. Now, however, trains which journeyed to and from Tokyo were spoken of, respectively, as 'up/down trains' (*nobori/kudari ressha*). The new capital was placed at the 'top'.

From the beginning, the role of Japanese railways was to reform a system based on inland water transportation and road carriage, and to promote the formation of an internal market, with far-reaching effects on the relationship of countryside and city. Chie Nakane gives a picture of the distribution of authority among feudal lords (the *Daimyô*) during the previous Tokugawa period:

One of the distinguishing characteristics was the clear-cut division between the urban and rural populations. The headquarters of the estate, where the Daimyô's castle was situated, had developed, in the course of time, into a town or city. This residential area of the Daimyô and his retainers (bushi) attracted merchants and craftsmen, while the rural areas were occupied only by peasants.[5]

4 Tetsuo Najita, Introduction, in T. Najita and J. Victor Koschmann (eds), *Conflict in Modern Japanese History: The Neglected Tradition*, Princeton University Press, 1982, p.16

5 Chie Nakane, *Kinship and Economic Organization in Rural Japan*, The Athlone Press London, 1967, p.44

The railway freed the movement of labour between regions, stimulated the movement of farmers into other industries, made possible the formation of a labour market centred in the cities, and opened up new possibilities of economic prosperity for the countryside. There was a struggle among older rural trade centres to have themselves located along the new network of railway tracks. One such struggle leads us directly to Tôson's depiction of the effects of these transformations on the countryside, because it took place between the people of the Ina Valley and the neighbouring Kiso Valley, in which Tôson's native town was located.

The dispute centred on plans for the development of the National Railways Central Trunk line (*kokutetsu chûô honsen*), which was to run from Shinjuku station in Tokyo, up through Nagano Prefecture where the two valleys are located. Kiso was finally chosen in 1894, and work on the line began in 1896. This victory was particularly vital for the Kiso Valley which was suffering severely from a loss of trade brought on by the collapse of the old landroute which had passed through the valley.

For some rural inhabitants at least, especially merchants, the railway was clearly a welcome innovation. With its promise of improved material conditions of life, it created an environment in the countryside of stimulated expectations as new as the atmosphere of Tokyo. For Tôson, however, the railway also bore with it an element of tragedy in its utter transformation of the countryside he once knew, described in his novel, *The Family* (*Ie*, 1911).

At the beginning of the book, the protagonist, Sankichi, visits the country home of his sister, Hashimoto Otane, and they take a walk together to the back of the house to view the terraced vegetable gardens and tilled land belonging to the family:

Midway up the slope they came to a garden of well-tended lilies, peas, and other plants, passed under a dark-green pumpkin trellis, and stepped into the garden where the old peasant was working. Along the stone wall ran a pleasant path with flowers, from which they could look down on the town in the valley.[6]

The peasant, placed unobtrusively among the 'pumpkins' and 'flowers', appears to be part of an unquestionable natural order; the same order that allows the relationship of clerks employed by the family to be described a few pages later as 'like that of feudal servants in the home of their master who had worked for the Hashimotos for two or three generations.'[7] The slow passage of time has allowed an intricate network of vegetable life to develop, and the peasant to find his proper place in a settled landscape. Though she does not go out much herself, Otane points out to her brother the house of some friends in the town below, confirming that the Hashimotos are also tied into the *human* network of the locality.

Towards the end of the book, after twelve years have past, Sankichi pays a second visit. A railway track is now being constructed through the very landscape he had once enjoyed:

himazaki Tôson, *The ily*, trans. Cecilia awa Seigle, Tokyo versity Press, 1976, p.5

id., p.2

*The sharply excavated, fresh red clay slope and the half-finished railroad crossing
the centre of the garden lay before his eyes. The miso storage and the white-
walled godowns with their loft windows under which he read Tatsuo's diary had
vanished. The pear garden, the grape arbour, the large stone well where the
maid Oharu had so often come to draw water – everything had been swept away.
Otane pointed with a broom at the devastated ruins of the garden. Only a small
log house still stood at the top of the opposite slope. A crew of workers arrived for
work under the cliff, carrying rail tongs on their shoulders.*[8]

The 'red clay slope', suggestive of a gash, not only disfigures the land, but
also speaks of a family wound: during the course of the novel, Otane's husband, Tatsuo, has run off with his mistress, leaving his wife destitute. Time-
honoured ties with the family, too, have been restructured so that, as
Tôson puts it, 'the relationship of the family and clerks was no longer one
of master to servants. Each now worked for a salary.'[9] The advantages of
the railway, in Tôson's eyes, are tempered by the substitution of a long-
standing and mutually beneficial dependency between people with the
impersonal and transferable feature of money exchange. This is a new economic order which has no space for a useless 'pleasant path with flowers'.

    I have already noted how events in Tôson's novels tend to
parallel details of his own life. In 1898, the author visited his real sister,
Sonoko, who was living in Kiso-Fukushima. He paid a second visit at the
end of Autumn in 1910. In the novel, we are told that Sankichi accompanied a family relative to a station where she was to take a train to Nagoya.
This must refer to the new station in Uematsu, opened on 5 October 1910,
and about five miles' walk from Kiso-Fukushima. The half-finished railroad he describes as being visible from the back garden is the track being
built to connect Uematsu to Kiso-Fukushima – the final link via the
Central Trunk line.

    Because Tôson was a member of that literate, land-owning
rural upper class which formed, in the Edo period, a kind of country gen-
try, it is understandable that he would lament the passing of the age at precisely the moment when the railway irrevocably tied his home district into
the new economy. It destroyed a social hierarchy which had served his family well. His father was the seventeenth successive head of the family to
hold the post of village headman (*shoya*). And until 1868, when Meiji began,
the Shimazaki house also served as the local *honjin* or officially designated
stopping place for the various feudal lords who made their way to and from

8 Ibid., p.284

9 Ibid., p.285

Edo during their alternate years of residence (the *sankin kôtai* system).

But if Tôson seems to confirm only the *negative* effects of the railway on his native place, I would like to suggest that he is not so far as he thinks from those local merchants. He too was able to benefit *positively* from the intrusion of the railway into his beloved rural landscape. The railway's construction through the back garden is final confirmation of a rupture in Tôson's experience of rural family life that had begun long before, and brought him to literary Tokyo. The break-up of the traditional household, like the railway, has both tragic and liberating aspects.

To return to Chie Nakane for a moment, the household was the primary unit of earlier social organisation in Japan:

In an agrarian community, a household has particularly important functions as a distinct body for economic management. A household ... is regarded as one distinct unit in society, represented externally by its head, and internally organised under his leadership. Once established a household is expected to remain intact in spite of changes of generations.[10]

In real life, the head of the family into which Tôson's sister married ran off with another woman, and he was also implicated in shady financial dealings which led to the family's ultimate bankruptcy. Not surprisingly, these events had a destabilising effect on his wife's mental state. A similar failure to 'remain intact in spite of changes of generations' also occurred in the history of Tôson's own Shimazaki family. After the death of the father through madness, headship of the household passed to Tôson's eldest brother, Hideo. Despite his good intentions, Hideo had a series of failed ventures and a spell in prison, until family members advised him to leave the country for Taiwan in 1906. In the case of both families, leadership was lacking, and led to a breakdown in this basic unit of rural social organisation. Even Tôson's relationship with his own wife was marred by his jealousy over a pre-marital affair of hers. It is not surprising that in the novel the hero's advice to his nephew who is struggling to make a living for himself is to 'forget about the responsibility you've inherited. Do what you can for yourself. That's enough.'[11]

Though he felt himself a member of sorts of the Yoshimura family which looked after him in Tokyo, he felt the separation from his true parents keenly. In his *When the Cherries Blossom*, we read how letters would come from the country home to the boy, Kishimoto, saying how things were bad at home and he should study hard in Tokyo:

Chie Nakane, op. cit., p.1

Shimazaki Tôson, *The ily*, op. cit., p.296

Privation and hardship seemed natural to him. He was never for a day able to forget the profound desire to keep other people in good humour, and find happiness for himself. The wilfulness of other youths who sat at their parents' knees and were able to do just as they liked was unknown to him.[12]

And, though Tôson seeks in his nostalgic writings to overcome the initial dislocation of his life by recapturing that first intimacy of country living, he has no option but to make that effort through a consciousness that has been profoundly transformed by his urban experience. He must somehow relocate his real family within 'himself'.

An indication of how even contact with the real family has become problematic once the transfer to the city is made can be found in the novel *Before the Dawn* (*Yoake mae*, 1929-35) in which the father, Hanzô, comes to visit his son, Wasuke, in Tokyo. Contrary to Hanzô's hopes, Wasuke now feels uncomfortable with the presence of his father in the city. He is acutely embarrassed, for instance, when his father, with his rural background and interest in Shinto, presents his school friend's mother with a simple mandarin orange instead of a gift more in keeping with sophisticated urban tastes, so that, 'even to contemplate the idea of some-one like his father being in the city seemed like an unbearable disharmony'.[13] This disharmony does not arise simply because of his father's physical presence in the city and ignorance of urban etiquette. Rather, the boy is uncomfortable with a discrepancy between his real family, embodied in the father, and the internalised image of that family that he has begun to construct for himself in its absence.

His wish seemed to be that his father should remain deep in the mountains of Kiso; by the hearth-side of the native home he should pass the days quietly in the company of his grandmother, his mother, and the servant Sakichi.[14]

The distinction between real and ideal can be explored further in *The Family* when Sankichi returns to the Tokyo home of his elder brother after his visit for the first time to his sister's. A photograph arrives from his sister of the whole family posing in the rural setting. The garden and the sunny slope that Sankichi witnessed for himself are in the background, suggesting the tranquillity of country life. The sight of the picture leads a family friend to remark: 'It must be lovely to live in a place like that, especially if you have the money,' to which the elder brother's wife replies: 'I agree. This is no life. Everything is just floating.'[15] Yet the book depicts the

12 Shimazaki Tôson, *Tôson zenshû*, op. cit., p.492

13 Ibid., vol.12, p.477

14 Ibid.

15 Shimazaki Tôson, *The Family*, op.cit., p.38

ultimate destruction of that tranquil country life.

We should bear in mind this suppression of reality in favour of idealisation when Sankichi is stimulated by the photograph before him to recall his earliest days with his original country family:

Pine trees and peonies grew in front of his father's study. On cold mornings, the family gathered round the sunken hearth in the floor and ate a local favourite, steaming roasted taro-and-buckwheat cakes dipped in grated turnip, blowing on them to cool them. In the evening an open fire burned, making the children's cheeks grow hot, while an old hired man making shoes out of straw told the stories of the will-o'-the -wisp deep in the mountains. The hearth held such pleasant memories.[16]

With the distancing effect of time, images may be recreated through the controlling prism of his own memories, and savoured without the threat of any intrusive reality. The way in which, in *When the Cherries Blossom*, the child's first arrival in Tokyo became, through repeated recollection, a safe and unthreatening memory, bears comparison here.

A passage from Tôson's series of descriptive essays, entitled *Chikuma River Sketches* (*Chikumagawa no suketchi*, 1912), seems to confirm that the writer is more concerned to seek out a countryside which fits his inner needs rather than to merely recreate the rural site based on actual memories. In search of a 'genuine' rustic experience, the narrator and his friend, W-, take a hike up the slopes of a nearby mountain where they intend to stay the night in a simple mountain hut. They are given a meal by the hut caretaker and his wife:

The caretaker comes to the entrance of the hut, saying, 'Will onions be all right with the beef?'
'Yes, onions will be just fine,' replies W- with a laugh.
'By the way, we've got potatoes too. Right! We'll put some potatoes in,' says the caretaker as he goes out. In a short while he returns with some of the onions and potatoes they have stored. We quickly gather around the open hearth, arranging the smoky wood fire with chopsticks and breaking up pieces of mountain beech to put into the hottest part. The blazing fire gives our faces a reddish cast.[17]

In both cases, the writer is describing an unabashed satisfaction of the senses that he found lacking in relations with the city family. What is remarkable in the latter passage, however, is not only a strong similarity with his recollections of the real family – the blazing fire, the red cheeks,

bid.

Shimazaki Tôson,
zuma River Sketches,
s. William E. Naff,
versity of Hawaii Press,
, p.70

the handling of hot food – but the fact that he is not actually describing his
own family at all. Tôson may have felt a rupture and disillusionment with
the reality of rural family life, but that does not stop the ideal family from
being a powerful image in his search for an unmediated rural experience.

The passage continues with a description of the relationship between the caretaker and his wife:

*He has a number of mannerisms: opening his mouth very wide when he speaks,
shaking his head, and laughing so hard that his tongue shows. The laugh is just
a bit on the crude side but its utter openness suits this cheerful young man. He
seems ready to do any kindness. His wife, already known for her industriousness,
is a plump, red-faced, black-haired, somehow girlish young woman. They seem
to be a perfectly matched couple.*[18]

The rustic simplicity of the father with his mandarin orange that jarred
against the tastes of the urbanised Wasuke becomes, in the ideal family, a
positive attribute as the hint of crudeness is more than compensated for by
the caretaker's magnanimity. What is more, by shifting to the ideal family,
Tôson is able to iron out the blemishes of reality. The 'perfectly matched
couple' are in stark contrast to the bad marriages of his own family. There
is, moreover, no threat of 'contamination' from the urban experience, with
the hut set apart even from the influence of the local rural town. As the wife
puts it, 'I was brought up in a lonely place but I've never been as lonely as I
was when I first came here.'[19]

The texts I have drawn on in this paper – *Chikuma River
Sketches, The Family , When the Cherries Blossom* and *Before the Dawn* – were
written at widely different times, ranging from 1900 to 1935. But my argument is not to suggest a gradual shift from some real to an ideal family over
a period of time. Rather, the rupture with the real countryside took place
in the earliest days of transfer to the city when Tôson was forced to 'find
happiness for himself'. From that point on, his recollections and writings
of the countryside were driven by his inner need for a site of security rather
than any literal depiction of the 'real' world, which, in any case, now lay
beyond his experience: the writer who was excluded from the site of familial intimacy at an early age has reinvented the family as an image of his own
making. He has thrown out the authority of the real family to become
author of his own memories.

Tôson begins with a forced detachment from family but
ends up regaining a form of control over the shape of his own environment

18 Ibid.

19 Ibid.

through his writing. And we can detect a similar manner in which the neg-
atively experienced intrusion of the railway is compensated by its
beneficial aspects. In *The Family*, we saw how the narrator lamented the
arrival of the railway because it led to a breakdown in established personal
relationships, specifically between family and servants. The implication
was that, now that servants worked simply for a salary rather than through
age-old ties, people had become less human than they were before.
However, just as that new class of local merchants was arising to take
advantage of a new more fluid economic situation in which – as Tôson
would have it – it was only the cold and interchangeable money transac-
tions that now mattered, the servants were in a position of greater control
over their own destinies, capable in theory at least to take their services
elsewhere. In Tôson's case, too, he may appear to speak entirely on behalf
of that earlier, now departed rural ideal, but his piecing together of what is
for him the most desirable version of the countryside from a mixture of
actual memory and fantasy in fact depends upon a very similar sense of
detachment and interchangeability.

  The destructive side of the railway he was at pains to depict
was an undeniable feature of the modern world he now inhabited.
However, the railway was also a material sign of a new economic order
emanating from the capital from which Tôson gained one form of power
even as he was denied another. For the same centralising force which had
brought him to the capital and deprived him of a full experience of the
native place was also the very means by which he was able to return home
on a path of rediscovery. This is true of course in the literal sense that he
can be easily transported back physically to his home town where he is then
able to lament its loss. But in a figurative way, too, the railway graphically
stands for a new Tokyo-centred social and economic hierarchy in which, as
a member of a new class of writers originally of the countryside but now
located within that centre, he is in a very fortunate position to give voice to
his own concerns, and speak on behalf of the countryside. With his own
early knowledge of country life, moreover, he is able to exploit a newly
emerging market need for nostalgic literary evocations of rural life. The
source of this new demand was partly due to the growing number of readers who lived in the city but yearned for what now appeared to be the simpler life of the native places which they, too, had left behind.

  Though Tôson may appear in his writings to be simply re-
creating the original countryside of his youth, that space is, in fact, gone

forever and can never be retrieved. Instead, the 'countryside' which concerns him is less a fixed locality than the articulation of a deeply felt need to find a site of plenitude and fulfilment in compensation for the loss he experienced in the city. He was certainly not the only urban dweller with a sense of dislocation, and who felt a need to reach back – if only in literary form – to the home town. The railway really does speak of his tragedy, his break from settled patterns, his disrupted memories. But it also offers a breaking free, a chance to put those fractured pieces together in a manner more to his liking, even if such an undertaking inevitably brings with it great loneliness. In any case, it cannot be denied that the railway is a sign of an historical rupture between past and present that has irrevocably transformed both urban and rural sites.

Hagiwara Hiroko

Tomiyama Taeko (1921–)
was born in Kobe and raised
in Manchuria where she first
witnessed the brutal
repression of people, an
experience that continues to
inform the subject matter of
her art.

Hagiwara Hiroko was born in
1951 and witnessed cultural
colonialism while growing up
near a US naval base in
eastern Japan. She is the
author of several books on
gender, race and art, and
lectures in Women's Studies
at Osaka Women's University.
She is a founding member of
the Asian Women and Art
Collective (AWAC).

Off The Comprador Ladder

Tomiyama Taeko's Work

The Korean women of Tomiyama Taeko's lithograph *Requiem for Dead Miners* stand straight, in grief and anger, in a dim gallery of the Maruki Museum. The gallery is lit by lanterns with paper shades on which Tomiyama printed Asian wild flowers and birds.

The Maruki Museum was founded by the painter-couple, Maruki Toshi and Maruki Iri, to show their own work *The Hiroshima Panels* and has a reputation for organising issue-raising exhibitions. *Tomiyama Taeko's Work in the Light of Lanterns* (November 1989), is the first exhibition to be organised after the museum's electricity supply was cut off (because of its refusal to pay the bills as a protest against nuclear power). Tomiyama's work becomes vivid in wavering dim light.

The Dragged and Divided

Heaps of coal waste loom large in her deep black lithographs. Shanty houses at the foot of the slag-heaps are deserted. Where have the miners gone? The slag-heaps of mining towns must have witnessed the core of the other history since 1910, when Japan started colonising Korea, up to the 1960s when energy policies shifted – from coal to oil. In Chikuho, a mining town in Kyushu, the southern island of Japan, many Korean miners worked and died in deep shafts, as in other mining towns, before the liberation of their country in 1945.

The lithograph portraying the slag-heaps of Chikuho and that of the Korean wives' grief are part of a series *The Dragged and Divided* (1980s). The film *Pop Out, Balsam Seeds! – On the Road to Chikuho and Korea* (dir. Tsuchimoto Noriaki), was produced in 1985 to show Tomiyama's work together with a piano accompaniment and a prose poem which narrates the Korean miners' fate.

The long winter came. Hailstorm raged and froze from treetops down to the ground.

In 1910 my country Korea became a Japanese colony and disappeared from the world map. Japanese officers came and hammered in stakes to enclose my field as their property. They also enclosed the forest where I had gathered firewood.

The railway was constructed on the land they requisitioned from my people.

Japanese troop trains started dashing through my people's land to Manchuria....

Recruiters came to the village and tempted my people who were starved in spite of the fact that they had worked from dawn till night.

'You will be fully fed in Japan.'

▼ Tomiyama Taeko, *The Dragged and Divided*, 1984, lithograph, photograph by Motohashi Seiichi

'You will have ample savings after three years work in Japan.'

They could only faintly expect to come back. They travelled away across the Sea of Genkai with one-way tickets to hell.

The war started. My people were now conscripted and taken to Japan across the sea to do forced labour at the bottom of Japanese society. Ih Ju Yol left his wife and five children behind. Chan Il Myon was torn from his newly married wife. Kim Gan Sok at the age of seventeen bade farewell to his mother. Thus I myself, too, came to Japan along with 700,000 Koreans.

Where am I? I am now in Chikuho, a mining town, where people say eight hundred and eight tunnels run under the ground….

Japanese coal mines became monstrous, sucking blood and crunching bones of poor miners, while wars were waged outside this country. How many miners were killed in tunnel collapses?

A fifteen-year-old miner cried, 'I am too starving to go on digging out coal.' He was beaten up with a wooden sword and pursued around in the tunnel by a site foreman. A roof suddenly caved in and killed him.

'Are we all going to be killed like this? Let's be beaten up together,' we swore, and carried the boy's body out of the shaft.

The film was produced to raise the issue of tormented Korean workers in the late 1930s. But for their slave labour, the imperialist economy could never have supported itself. And though the Japanese Empire was ruined in 1945, the economic success of post-war Japan was neither a miracle nor an accident. It was based on organised labour management which had evolved in the process of colonial labour How many Koreans were conscripted to Japan? Where, how and by whom they were recruited and transported? What about their working conditions, their whereabouts and their lives after the war? The series of lithographs *The Dragged and Divided* and the film, which makes the series more accessible, show Tomiyama's historical consciousness and convince audiences of the urgency for an historical investigation.

Coal mining was one of the key industries which played a prominent role in the post-war economic boom in Japan. When Tomiyama started visiting mining towns in the 1950s, a story of dead Korean miners was only told through 'people's secret talk. While the war produced all kinds of ravages in Korea the mining towns were still busy producing coal. Coal mining has always been based on miners' sacrifice. As the slag-heaps became larger, rain made the river run higher and caused a flood. When water ebbed away, farmers found their fields unarable due to the minerals left by the flood. The farmers deserted their land and came to the mining towns to become miners at low wages. Skilled miners were dismissed when their wages became too high for the companies to continue to pay. The companies scrimped on pit props because one pit prop was more expensive than a miner's life, roof-collapses were unavoidable and even calculated.

What Tomiyama saw and heard in the mining towns led her on a dedicated quest. How is art possible when massive injustices and inequalities are maintained? What should artists express in that society? How could she produce art which miners could fully share? The series *The Dragged and Divided* was achieved after an unyielding and painstaking search for the 'other' history the and 'other' way of art.

From Manchuria in colonial days

▲ Tomiyama Taeko, *Dictator*, 1980, lithograph, photograph by Motohashi Seiichi

Tomiyama, now in her seventies, has always been concerned to produce people's art as 'live charcoal in the snow'. This is a saying of Mao Tse Tung who criticised bourgeois art as 'flowers on a glittering brocade.' In her autobiography with the same title as the film, *Pop Out, Balsam Seeds! – A Quest for Art and Life* (1983) she confesses that in her teens Van Gogh, Gauguin and Cezanne were her deities.

Tomiyama grew up as a daughter of a Japanese employee of Dunlop Rubber in Manchuria, which Japan colonised. Young, unskilled typists from Britain were paid eight times more than her father, an experienced accountant. Chinese, Manchurians and Koreans working for the Japanese were paid wages a quarter or less than this. 'I was the daughter of a pseudo-Westerner, employed by the British, working for them in a lesser status, assimilating their values and exploiting other Asians. That was what Japan was.' Seeing this finely layered comprador ladder from her problematic position as a Japanese, she was further suffocated as a woman. In those days, when Fascism stressed the virtue of the National Mother, what could be expected of a woman other than that she should be a good mother and virtuous wife? For a Japanese girl, suffocating in the colonial days in Manchuria under Japanese Fascist rule, it was natural to yearn for the *avant-garde*, Post-Impressionist 'heroes of a far away, imagined Europe'. Dadaism, Russian Constructivism and German Expressionism had not yet reached her.

She came to Tokyo to study art in 1938. Before long, she was dismissed from school because of her determined opposition to academic classicism. After leaving school she was involved with a small group of modernist painters.

When Japan opened hostilities against the US and Britain   **No way out** major painters were organised into the Imperial Artists' Association and patronised by the Fascist government. From Japan's ambivalence about Western art, its yearning and inferiority complex, the government turned to nationalist artists to serve as commissioned war painters; painters who remained independent of the association were in poverty. Tomiyama, as a painter without recognition, was as poor as the latter. But she could not condone vagabond heroism financially supported by their wives' sweated work. A woman who was married to a liberal artist was meant to give up her own career (an artist's career in many cases) and to take full responsibility for family life. Female altruism, which had long been encouraged by Confucian patriarchy, thus supported the fantasised ideals of male artists. To be an artist Tomiyama has remained unmarried but, in any case, her hand-to-mouth existence in wartime and in the post-war period did not allow her to paint.

While looking after the two children, who she intentionally parented as a single mother, she started travelling to the mining towns. Her Cezanne-like landscape in oils during those turbulent days will not be shown. Only a small, black-and-white reproduction, with which the autobiography is illustrated as her historical record, tells of contradictions she grappled with in the mining towns. Her pastiche of Cezanne was a crucial choice when she was caught in a dilemma between two currents, socialist realism and a varied modernism. The former was monotonously sloganistic and in fact indifferent to workers' lives. Tomiyama could not sympathise with those painters who served a political party and seemed servile to the changing Western influences. Neither American Abstract Expressionism nor Pop Art, (so far as an artist in Japan could know in the 1950s) was related to the miners' reality. The miners asked the city-bred woman painter why she had come to a mining town from Tokyo and whether she would make a living by selling her paintings of the mines to the bourgeoisie. How, what, and for whom should she paint?

In her book *Aesthetics for Liberation – What the Twentieth Century Artists Challenged* (1979), Tomiyama examines the contemporary

Western *avant-garde* which had inspired her: Dadaism, Russian Constructivism, Käthe Kollwitz, Otto Dix, the Bauhaus, the New Deal Art Movement, and early Surrealism. But she knew she could not find a way out of her dilemma by imitating Goncharova, Kollwitz or Ben Shahn. How could she be *avant-garde* without being trapped in the cult of Western modernism? Traditional Japanese painting could never be an alternative for her. It was retrogressive and stagnant in its decorativeness. It had dominated the Japanese art scene for hundreds of years as a flower on a glittering brocade.

From mining towns

▲ Tomiyama Taeko,
*Demons of Post Colonial
Power*, 1978, collage,
photograph by
Motohashi Seiichi

In 1961 Tomiyama herself, like a balsam seed of the title of her autobiography leaped out and boarded a ship bound for Buenos Aires via India and South Africa. It was not a journey of hope but an escape from a deadlock she had reached after dedicated involvement, as an artist and activist, in a struggle against the rationalisation of the mining industries.

The rationalisation policy for 110,000 miners, presented by the fourteen biggest mining companies in 1959 had led to a nationwide struggle: capitalist versus labour. The united capitalists would never concede a struggle which would affect a campaign against the renewal of the Japan US Security Treaty scheduled for the next year. The treaty was about American military bases in Japanese territory and Japanese rear support. The treaty could be denied its renewal since the Japanese majority was against perpetuation of post-war military occupation and any militarisation. But the US contemplated raising its armaments in the West Pacific area to build up a fort-like chain of bases around unstable Korea and Vietnam. And Japanese capitalists anticipated advancement to the status of a first-class economic power by impetuous and coercive policies. The miners' unions lost their struggle against rationalisation. Tomiyama was, in both ways, defeated.

Having ceased to be useful, the miners disappeared from the scene. The deserted slag-heaps in her lithographs remind me of her journey to South America by sea to trace the Japanese miners who had emigrated to Brazil, Chile and Bolivia. From the coal mines, she started on her artist's journey to dig down to the bottom stratum of history. In the autobiography she describes her observations and reflections on poverty and inequalities in the Third World. She confirmed that what she had seen in the mining towns was part of a global institutionalised injustice. But she could not stop questioning herself as to whether her journeys, not only the one to Buenos Aires but also to the mining towns, had been sentimental – sightseeing exotic poverty.

In the 1970s when she encountered the Korean poet Kim Chi Ha's work, which cuttingly and humorously reproached the Japanese government's intervention in South Korea, Tomiyama would have discerned a kindred spirit of sharp historical consciousness and expression. Kim Chi Ha was a poet whose work caused his detention.

Kim Chi Ha, the poet

  In 1976 she contributed lithographs to a 15-minute television programme *Kim Chi Ha, a Christian in Darkness*. Kim's trial was scheduled to be held soon after. The programme was not broadcast on the grounds that it might harm international friendship and the television station peddled the view that the control was self-imposed. But the rejected programme was re-made into a series of slides with music and shown widely, including the US and Mexico.

  Faced with rejection by the mainstream media and impressed by possibilities of slide presentation, Tomiyama started a one-woman studio, *Hidané* (kindling charcoal), to produce a slide film of her paintings and lithographs. Sympathetic friends organised a small group for distribution, *Group Fuigo* (bellows), to blow about her work and Kim Chi Ha's poems.

The first slide presentation was *Chained Hands in Prayer – Korea, 1974* (1977), which consists of 140 slides of her lithographs from the series 'For Kim Chi Ha and his Poems'. Mortification (1974), which is the central poem in the presentation, was written in prison and published in the following year when the poet, who had been sentenced to death, was miraculously released thanks to international campaigns. The following passage awakened Tomiyama:

Chained Hands in Prayer

▶ Tomiyama Taeko, *A Memory of the Sea*, 1986, oil on canvas, photograph by Motohashi Seiichi

▼ Tomiyama Taeko, *Galungan Festival Night*, 1986, oil on canvas, photograph by Motohashi Seiichi

*We were sentenced to death. I laughed. Kim Byon Kon started his final
statement. 'I am honoured', he said. 'What does it mean? Is a man to say
honoured when he is sentenced to death?' Then, all of a sudden, I felt myself in a
raging storm swaying my whole soul. Is that a saying of a saint? Are we saints?
Yes, we won at last. We won against the threat of death.*

*We had been chained flesh. But we now stared at a flare of true life which had
just blazed up in our souls. We were inspired with the overwhelming beauty of
the lively flare. The moment of blazing up was our historical moment. That was
not only worldly pleasure but eternal and spiritual pleasure. And I must say we
were also in the perfect pleasure of art.*

*Then certain words flashed into my mind: 'Political Power of Imagination'. A
pain pierced me. 'Political Power of Imagination!' The words imprinted on my
mind meant true unification of politics and art. Not at all dubious eclecticism.
Unification! Unification! At long last I pleasurably overcame such a maddening
and unmanageable gap between my stance as one of the people, my political
activity and artistic expression.*[1]

Tomiyama found a comrade who had, like her, suffered from that gap and
now overcame it. While 'Political Power of Imagination' meant, for the
detained poet, a glorious moment of collective honour and victory of
chained prisoners at the court of death sentence, it meant for the Japanese
artist, a new language and direction for her art:

*We will make art into an agent of change, change for human liberation, by
breaking through national barriers, disturbing the division of professionals and
non-professionals, and removing walls between genres. We now examine the way
of art. Art has become nothing but a commercial product dealt with by art
dealers, collectors and mass media. In this whole capitalist society we still hope to
find out and produce a new way of art while we work out a new collectivity
between artists and public in a struggle.*

Tomiyama stopped showing her work in commercial galleries (in the so-
called rental galleries, which form well over half of Japan's active contemporary art galleries). She had found it hard to reconcile herself to their
intolerance of even a touch of politics and so the slide presentation was
shown in alternative spaces. The question of audience/buyers had hitherto
been problematic for the artist; her work had been appreciated by a limited
audience, those visiting a gallery in Tokyo. But now she could reach a wider
audience because the artist herself, like a troubadour, could take the work,

1 Kim Chi Ha,
Mortification, 1974

which was more portable and accessible, to her audiences. Tomiyama's images of Korean people and Japanese power are allegorical and sarcastic. Her work is not an illustration of the poems, but the two artists' works are complementary. Kim's poetry is vivified by her images.

Internationally, when a great deal of criticism was being raised against the Korean government's treatment of political offenders, *Chained Hands in Prayer* was shown in Britain, France, the US, Mexico and secretly in the Philippines. In Thailand a pirate edition in a book form was published.

Kim Chi Ha was imprisoned again, due to publication of the above poem, on the grounds that he offended against the Anti-Communist Law. Tomiyama went on producing Korean pieces, responding to Kim's outrageous poetry which criticised Japan's long-lasting control over the Korean peninsula. Some of the poems were banned in South Korea. Two slide presentations dealt with the issue of contemporary Korea-Japan connections. *Wild Rumour* (1979), with Kim Chi Ha's poems and *Prayer in Memory, Kwangju, May 1980* (1980) produced soon after the Kwangju uprising.

Prayer in Memory   After the assassination of President Park, whose military regime had consolidated its domination with the support of the US and Japan, remnants of the dictator's circle fought among themselves to maintain their vested interests. 100,000 people rose up in Seoul to demand for lifting the martial law. The troops were dispatched to suppress the people's revolt. Against that military violence, in Kwangju, the southern state of South Korea, people organised street demonstrations. But the military brutality, led by Lieutenant General Chun Du Hwan resulted in carnage. Prayer in Memory tells us of these assaults. A pregnant woman was stabbed, her stomach ripped open and the unborn baby thrown at her. Tomiyama portrays the killed woman who will never be silenced: given a lasting and vocal figure by the artist. Tomiyama also portrays women with joyful, shining faces who could also be seen on the street for a short time, in the very early period of the uprising.

Since this piece Korean women's varied images have appeared more than ever in Tomiyama's work: peddling vegetables, working in co-operation with each other, mourning their children's deaths, standing still, roaring with laughter, and shouting out, demanding humane treatment. Apart from the image of the exotic Korean beauty, Korean women used to be regarded as inappropriate for art and images of working-class Korean women rarely appear in Japanese artists work. . The philanthropic gaze is the first to avoid and Tomiyama is working within a paradox, conscious that she is of the other whom she is portraying and yet, she is not one of them. While she sympathised with Korean women (as one of the oppressed), as a Japanese, she cannot easily sing the same song together with the oppressed in Korea. Tomiyama's Korean women reject our direct identification with them as the oppressed, and yet they do include an occasional smile that seems to invoke a soroptimist solidarity. It is Japanese woman's double-sided position as an aggressor/victim that is examined by the artist.

Tomiyama moved to colourful, oil painting in the mid-1980s. In the year of the fiftieth anniversary of the Japanese **A Memory of the Sea** war against Asian and Pacific countries she painted *A Memory of the Sea*. This is part of her series raising the issue of Japan's responsibility in war. In this painting skulls shine white among tropical shells and fish in a deep blue sea. The bones of Asian people who were utilised, exploited, raped and killed by Japanese power/people are piled up. Their luminescent bones recount the lives of each of the wartime victims – now at the bottom of the Pacific. The piece reminds me of the Mexican skulls of Posada.

The slide presentation *A Memory of the Sea – A Dedication to the Korean Military Comfort Women* (1986), consists of oil paintings, lithographs and a poem, accompanied by Asian music. This presents her feminist view of the Pacific war, naked women exposed to the gaze of Japanese soldiers. But this is more than a metaphor of war: the Japanese Imperial Army officially organised the Military Comfort Women, many of whom were Korean, who served the soldiers sexually. When the war was over, those who were survived were doubly discriminated against: either because they were Koreans in Japan, or because they were perceived as unclean (prostitutes) in their own, liberated country. In 1991 a Korean Comfort Woman first revealed to the public the commitment of the Japanese government to this. Military Comfort Women numbered some 100,000, or even 200,000 and historical investigation is expected. But so far the affair has been rubbed out of history. Tomiyama stresses that Confucian ideology of women's chastity has put the women to silence for over forty years and

the Japanese government has welcomed this silence.

Slide presentation has changed Tomiyama's, working practice and pieces are painted in order to be made into slide presentations. Parts of Tomiyama's paintings are successively brought into focus and projected onto the screen: in darkness the imperial chrysanthemum is glaring in yellow; pink genitals are uncovered. To juxtapose the imperial symbol and the destroyed naked female figures is a raid into iconographic taboo. Audiences are led to face what the war destroyed and spoiled, and who should not evade responsibility.

◀ Tomiyama Taeko, *Let's Go To Japan*, 1989, oil on canvas, photograph by Hara Kazuo

After the exhibition in Maruki Museum, Tomiyama completed a series, *Let's Go To Japan*. A Kawasaki motor cycle dashes towards us, overloaded with colourful, Asian masks. East, South, and South-East Asians flocking to Japan in the hope of making money in the economic giant of the Far East. The Japanese government has not yet laid out a clear policy on foreign workers and discussion swirls interminably about whether, and to what extent, non-skilled foreign workers should be allowed to work. Asians are now working in bad conditions Japanese people would not tolerate. Also the flow of traffic in women from South Korea, the Philippines and Thailand to Japan has been established. Tomiyama asks herself what has changed? The Japanese have always exploited other Asians' labour and sex. Asians (the word conventionally indicates Asians other than Japanese) in Japan are regarded as a problem and have not yet debunked the auto-toxaemic myth of the racially homogeneous nation, Japan.

Off the Comprador Ladder

The last slide presentation, *The Thai Girl Who Never Came Home* (1992), is a collective work with Thai and Japanese artists. The woman painter Jarassri Rupcamdee and the boys' band Carawan, participated from Thailand. The work is about a woman who came to Tokyo from a rural Thai village to be a prostitute. It could not have been completed but for a common understanding among the artists about sexual exploitation and the economic differentials between the two countries. Such a collective work with other Asian artists is rarely realised, or even dreamt of, by Japanese artists in general.

In Japan, where patriarchal Confucianism and women's altruism are pervasive in alliance with modern capitalist sexism and racism as well as the cult of valorised Western culture, Tomiyama's life-long quest for people's art and an Asian Feminist identity is surrounded by crucial factors. Her work is often called political art. The Western-made myth of 'art for art's sake' was imported into Japan in the last decades of the nineteenth century, and is still functioning to sanitise the gallery, sweeping away any touch of politics. What Tomiyama has searched for is not political art as illustration of a certain dogma which exists outside art. Her interests are not 'art and society' nor 'artists and social situations' which political artists are usually expected to be conscious about. Here the items follow the word and are replaceable, and art and the other items are regarded independent from one another. That is the very idea that Tomiyama has confronted. Kim Chi Ha's idea on art/politics, the 'political power of imagination' as a collective achievement is suggestive.

Tomiyama's quest for an Asian feminist identity is about collectivity. The word 'identity', against the Western notional 'self', does not mean something solid with a frozen core and clear boundary demarcating an individual exclusive of others. An identity is originally not personal but, for better or worse collective, based on class or race, gender or sexuality. The artist finds it hard to break through collective national identity ('we the Japanese'). This monolithic identity, barring other potential identities, is backed by obsessions about the universality of the West and the backwardness of Asia. Western art has functioned as the powerful tool to consolidate the notion of the hierarchy, in the middle of which Japan should be positioned. She is the artist who is walking out of that obsessive identity and searching for a new collectivity with other Asian women by looking closely at Japanese imperialism, the curse of which is working on women all the more.

Lisa Reihana

Lisa Reihana is a Maori film and video maker based in Christchurch, New Zealand. Her videos include *Wog Features* and *Tauira*.

Skinflicks

Practices in Contemporary Maori Media

Brief and biased history

New Zealand was first settled by voyagers from the islands of East Polynesia. They lived here for a thousand years before seafarer capitalists reached these shores. Colonisation by the British and other Europeans was imminent as New Zealand provided a rich bounty of resources. The term *maori*[1] came into usage around 1850 when racial difference required definition. *Maori* means normal, usual, ordinary and was used in relation to the 'other' culture at this time, the *Pakeha* colonisers.

The unique *Maori/Pakeha* situation is shown by the existence of a treaty drawn up to define land and resource rights. The Treaty of Waitangi was signed in 1840 by representatives for the Crown and some chiefs of various tribes throughout New Zealand. It contains three articles that ensure equality in distribution of resources between *Maori* and *Pakeha*. The treaty had two translations – one in English, the other in *Maori*. The meaning of the two translations is perceived differently, this has created animosity between the people of New Zealand. This language dispute represents the tip of many cultural and philosophical differences.

As a result of the misinterpretation of the treaty, *Maori* are in a substantially weaker position than *Pakeha*. *Maori* suffer detrimentally in areas of health, housing, prison and in education. Some *Maori* have since been asserting *Tino Rangatiratanga*, that is, reclaiming sovereign rights as the first people of this land. A growing voice of discontent is demanding that the treaty be fully upheld, using the legal systems that created the document. The struggle to regain an acceptable repayment for the losses since 1840 continues.

It was thought by many *Pakeha* that *Maori* would become an

A Dictionary of the Maori Language, H.W. Williams, h edition, GP Books, ellington, 1971

extinct people through war and introduced diseases. The focus over the last 150 years has been that of survival. *Maori* have been struggling to maintain an identity as a progressively landless people. A need for work saw an urban

drift into the cities beginning in the 1940s. This move led to detribalisation, a loss of identity and of power. During the 1970s *Maori* radicalism evolved, a seeking of identity and a new consciousness developed. Urban *marae* provided a space for people of all tribes to practice traditional values, as well as new ones.

▲ *That's the Beat*
Rongotai Lomas

It is within this context, as an oppressed people, that *Maori* filmmakers have been operating. Since the 1970s the themes often address issues of land rights, effects of colonisation and exploration of origins. The opportunities for *Maori* filmmakers to develop have been limited, but there have always been *Maori* working within the industry. In the 1990s, an ever increasing number of *Maori* and Polynesian are now producing our own stories.

Political correctness   There has been pressure from within government to recognise what is unique to New Zealand's cultural identity. The

▶ *Sister Bestial*
Fear Brampton
Mark Summerville

response has been policies termed bi-culturalism. The meaning of bi-culturalism varies from group to group. Some *Maori* perceptions include seeing bi-culturalism as another form of government assimilation; and as an unequal policy which in practice is compulsory for *Maori* and optional for *Pakeha*. Bi-culturalism has had positive effects. All government agencies and some private organisa-

tions are educating their employees to understand and incorporate a *Maori* dimension into the workplace. So many New Zealanders have raised their awareness. Unfortunately, this interest is not reflected by the State-owned broadcasters.

Financial support   New Zealand is a small country with limited resources. The government bodies specifically supporting our film and video industry are the New Zealand Film Commission, New Zealand On

Air and the Creative Film and Video Fund of the QEII Arts Council. These bodies acknowledge the need to fund more *Maori*-based projects.

New Zealand on Air funds Radio Broadcasting, Television and Independent projects. Its Mission Statement:

To develop the distinctiveness, variety and quality of New Zealand broadcasting that reflects the culture and identity of all New Zealanders under the Treaty of Waitangi.[2]

New Zealand on Air requires broadcast commitment before the funding of television projects is granted. Gaining broadcast commitment is no easy task, more difficult is to ensure a good screening time. Television New Zealand is our only viable financial broadcaster, this allows institutional gatekeeping systems to block what may or may not be produced in New Zealand. Situations arise where *Pakeha* production companies and independent *Maori* filmmakers compete for the same funding. This often results in the established companies dominating the funding rounds.

In 1991 New Zealand On Air created the Music Video Fund, NZ$5000 is matched by the record company of the recorded artists. Music Videos provide an important outlet for *Maori* and *Pakeha* filmmakers. Also in 1991, NZ$4.5 million of $38.4 million was allocated to *Maori*

Television. This translates to 130 hours broadcast time out of 1000 hours funded. Programmes which involved *Maori* programme-makers in the production of television programmes which promote *Maori* language and culture for a *Maori* audience received $5,625,900 from New Zealand On Air funding. An objective of this organisation is to apply at least 6 per cent of the net Public Broadcasting revenue, net of collection costs, to *Maori* Broadcasting.

The filmmakers obtain maximum grants of up to NZ$7000, and up to NZ$30,000 for established directors. Experimental

filmwork is encouraged by new and established directors. The fund has
come under increasing pressure as most directors have to receive grants
from this fund before applying to the New Zealand Film Commission.

**Screening
opportunities**
New Zealand theatres rarely screen short films prior to feature films. This limits possible outlets since the bulk of New
Zealand films are produced in the short-film format. The screening of
short films is generally as a curated package. The Creative Film and Video
Fund actively promote experimental film packages of New Zealand and
International work. These screenings are special events and often occur as
a 'one night only' chance for audiences to view. *Maori* film screenings have
been, and continue to be held on *marae*. The viewing of film by a *Maori*
audience, particularly on *marae*, can be a very different experience from
that of a city theatre. Merata Mita describes a rare screening of archival
footage :

*Maori audiences proclaim the passing of their number who appear in any film,
before or during the screening, often very loudly. Film screenings are always
treated as an event, particularly when they are held on the marae in a more*

▲ *Bastion Point – Day 507*
Merata Mita

*Maori context. There, the nature of the screening changes to one of more direct
interaction, on a more intimate level within an audience that is also a community
under pressure.*[3]

It is a courtesy gesture, often practised by *Maori* film crews,
to premiere a work to the people or tribe whose image and stories have been
collected. Some directors feel that all the footage collected by a crew should
be returned to that tribe so they can retain their own history where it is most
relevant, create their own archives.

In 1990, I began presenting packages of experimental films

3 Jonathan Dennis and Jan
Bieringa (eds), *Film in
Aotearoa*, p.39

4 Hours counted from *The
Listener*, 19 December 1992

by *Maori* directors. The directors screened in packages since 1990 includes; Fear Brampton and Mark Summerville, Rewia Brown, Rachel Churchward, Grant Fell, Robert Jahnke, Rongotai Lomas, Merata Mita, Joanna Paul, Karen Sidney and Chris McBride, Television New Zealand's *Maori* Department and Tim Worrall. These screenings were curated to contextualise my own work, and to increase the accessibility and promote what I consider to be the most interesting filmwork in New Zealand at present. The presentations *Maori Media Images* held at the Australian Centre for Photography, Sydney, *Titiro Ngaa Pakoko* at the Wellington City Art Gallery have occurred within an institutional context. This can deter an indigenous audience from attending. *Visions From Aotearoa – Maori Commitment to Film* was held at Boomalli Aboriginal Artist Ko-operative in Sydney. This venue was appropriate, allowing the Aboriginal community a venue in which to voice their questions and concerns.

New Zealand Broadcasting

Apart from three hours in a possible three hundred and seventy-nine each week,[4] and the rare *Maori* documentary, New Zealand media is Eurocentric in its programming. Television New Zealand's locally produced programmes include soap operas, game shows, news and sport. New Zealanders are therefore 'treated' to imported American, English and Australian material. Overseas material is cheap to air, but this 'cost effective' exercise does not foster or enrich a cultural perception of ourselves. This reinforces *Pakeha* insecurity and creates a lack of confidence in our own culture. A danger exists for *Maori* if issues are restricted to one programme and time-slot. If tokenism is to be truly avoided, *Maori* issues need to be addressed across the spectrum; in drama, documentary as well as in our own specialist programmes. Non-*Maori* and *Maori* communicators are in the process of redressing this imbalance. There is a wealth of material, and it is time the indigenous people of Aotearoa tell the stories in our own ways.

Te Manu Aute

Te Manu Aute is a collective that acknowledges communication as a common element. *Te Manu Aute* embraces film and video makers, radio broadcasters, dancers, writers and musicians. *Te*

Manu Aute was the first organisation to lobby the government for a quota of *Maori* material on mainstream television. *Te Manu Aute* publish a quarterly newsletter under the same name.

A huge achievement inseminated by *Te Manu Aute* was the *E Tipu E Rea* series later administered under the *Te Manuka* Film Trust. Debated and developed over four years, this series of five, half-hour dramas was an important breakthrough. For the first time the combined talents of *Maori* writers, directors and crew worked together in a supportive atmosphere. Made in 1989 the series included; *Eel* directed by Joanna Paul, *Roimata* written and directed by Riwia Brown, *Thunderbox* directed by Lee Tamahori, *Te Moemoea* directed by Rawiri Paratene and *Variations On A Theme* directed by Don Selwyn.

Independant moves

Independent filmmakers provide an important balance to what cannot be produced by mainstream television. *Marae*, screened Sunday mornings on Television New Zealand, provides an important outlet for independent work. However, access to mainstream television continues to limit screening opportunities by institutional gate-keeping systems. Alternatives are developing to address specific *Maori* needs. *Maori* tribal broadcaster *Tainui* Television covered the 1992 *Aotearoa Maori* Festival held in February, 1992. This event was screened on both Television New Zealand and TV3, an historical first. Eventually, *Tainui* Television would like to see UHF frequencies throughout New Zealand operated by the local tribal groups.

▶ *Savage Rites*
Tim Worrall

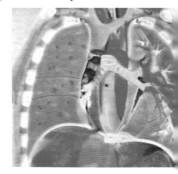

Television New Zealand's *Maori* Department

It has been a long battle to bring the *Maori* dimension to the New Zealand public. Broadcasting in the mainstream has increased *Maori* visibility to the general public. The screening times of the work produced by the *Maori* Department has been a contentious issue. Screening times do not reflect the working demographics of its target audience. The *Maori* news *Te Karere* began screening on New Zealand television for four minutes in 1983 *Te Karere* now goes to air for ten minutes from 5.15pm. Many New Zealanders finish work at 5.30pm or

later, the viewing of this programme by the employed is very difficult. *Marae* plays Sunday mornings from 10am – 12am, when many *Maori* are often attending spiritual services.

Television New Zealand's *Maori* Department has a team of dedicated workers. The main body of their work is produced for *Marae*. *Marae* has a format reflecting the spiritual values of *Maori*. The *marae* is the area in front of the meeting house where *Maori* gather to *korero*, it is this concept of a place to speak and air issues, that gives the show its title.

Each week a *Karakia* by a priest opens the show, the denomination changes from week to week. This is an inclusive gesture that recognises and respects difference. Opening titles follow and then *Waka Huia* a half- or one-hour documentary. Generally a *kuia* or *kaumatua*, who are an important focus for the *marae* because they link the old ways with the present, is interviewed. *Waka Huia* can have an unmediated feel with editing being as unobtrusive as possible. Information can include traditional planting techniques, personal stories and tribal history. This is one way to create an archive of our elders. The problem is that the ownership of footage belongs to this market-driven and indifferent corporation. Usually *Waka*

Huia is filmed in the *Maori* language. *Waka Huia* has received complaints for not sub-titling by non-*Maori* speakers who are denied access to the few programmes with *Maori* content. The practicalities for the *Maori* department is that it operates on a limited budget.

Included within the *Marae* hour is a magazine style community noticeboard, an edited round up of *Te Karere* the weekly *Maori* news and *Tagata Pasifica*, the Pacific Island news and events outlet. The inclusion of which recognises our geographic position in the Pacific region, and our entwined ancestry.

**Training
opportunities**
Although there are limited training opportunities, an increasing number of *Maori* are attending media courses at universities and polytechnics. A problem is there are no permanent *Maori* lecturers. This lack of role models to provide a balanced perspective leaves a predominantly Eurocentric art view. Short-term appointments at universities have been made in the past, but until an ongoing commitment to employ more than one *Maori* lecturer in each organisation is made, specifically *Maori*, but also *Pakeha* students will remain uncatered to.

However, some *Maori*-based training groups have operated. *He Taonga a Waiatarau*, was a training course for *Maori* and Pacific Islanders. This course ran for five years and provided an important training ground for many who are still working in the industry today. *He Taonga a Waiatarau* recognised *Maori* learning structures, run at Freemans Bay Community Centre on a *marae* basis, it integrated traditional and spiritual values into the course. Problems were experienced by some female students who felt they were being relegated to the stereotypical working roles in film crews.

Another training opportunity was a one-off scheme called *Kimihia*. It was run for one year by Television New Zealand, fifty *Maori* had the opportunity to train 'in the field'. As media training for *Maori* is a new

▲ *More Fool You*
Rachel Churchward

area, there were problems as the learning process evolved. Some personal experiences included suspicion of *Kimihia* as a guilt-assuaging exercise by Television New Zealand, alienation from working in a large and hierarchic structure, as well as institutional racism. *Kimihia* trainees based in Auckland had a support base in the *Maori* Department, trainees based in the smaller centres felt they were working in a void. Some trainees were later employed by Television New Zealand, others have continued to work as independent filmmakers.

Experimental filmmaking

The number of *Maori* and Pacific Island directors creating experimental short films is very small. These new filmmakers are a de-tribalised and urbanised generation informed by their cultural background, and who extend traditional concepts and artistic forms into new areas. A growing sense of self is apparent in these works; questioning dominant Eurocentric history, exploring gender issues, and sexual preferences. It is important to stress the diversity of concerns and styles, to dispel the myth of a recognisable '*Maori* style'. The decision to use non-linear narratives is a cultural and political gesture. The rejection of mainstream storytelling as inappropriate to the meaning. The use of experimental narratives, poeticism and allusion allow these filmmakers to discover and create a unique voice.

Rongotai Lomas, Ngati Hikairo of Tainui, is our techno-funky *Maori* image creator. Graduating from the Film Department of Canterbury University he further trained at the National Film Unit and in Television New Zealand's Graphics Department. Lomas's film *Armature of Bone*, a 16-mm black-and-white cerebral exploration used a skeleton and a television with continually rolling bars in a lone warehouse. A feeling of angst pervades the film reflecting the early 1980s Punk movement.

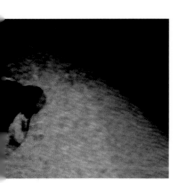

Armature of Bone has continued to be a source of images for self-appropriation and re-stylisation by Lomas. These and other images were used in a one-hour performance *Solvent*, a collaboration with George Hubbard and Tone Cornaga. Performed at Artspace Gallery, *Solvent* incorporated projected video, live and pre-recorded sound. Incorporating text, 'monoculturalism' is overlaid and repeated, this created a structure built of words, a reference to the treaty and the current state of race relations in *Aotearoa*. A sensory overload, *Solvent* was aimed at today's urban and inner-city population. Offering no solutions it reflects the mood of discontent.

Lomas has made music videos for local *Maori* rap bands *Upper Hutt Posse* and *Chain Gang*. The rap format is subverted for its *Maori* audience, the voice of discontent is offset by placing images of ourselves in the media. This allows self confidence to grow and acceptance of *Maori* as a natural part of New Zealand culture. Drawing on knowledge gained while working in the graphics department, Lomas's work uses dense visual layers and incorporates sophisticated, computer-generated images. Strongly based on inner-city street culture, dancing outside the

McDonalds in Auckland's Queen Street (a hangout for young *Maori* and Poynesians), these images reflect an identity they are creating. Lomas has also used young schoolkids amongst the local music stars, he provides role models who are within reach.

Mark Summerville and Fear Brampton, Te Aupouri and Te Rarawa, have collaborated on many projects since meeting at Elam Art School at Auckland University. Their first video *Homosensual* is set on a beach, following the movements of a man walking on sand and sitting amongst bushes. This relatively mundane subject is enlivened through video posterisation, altering the image into a seductive display of splendid colours requiring close watching to decipher the content. *Homosensual* contains elements that are further explored in later works.

Summerville and Brampton's work is characterised by the poetic in both visual opulence and aural soundscapes. Their work is characterised by an elemental concern containing wind, fire, and earth as central to the narrative. The use of *Maori* and Pacific icons, materials and actors places this work firmly in the South Pacific context. Gay issues are central, but not in an obvious way because this position is a given, there is no pandering to being the 'other'.

Singing Seas is a luscious evocation of gods both Polynesian

and Greek. It speaks of love in mythological proportions. Primal, elemental, it has a classical look and atmospheric sound. The soundtrack adds an important dimension and gives the film a timelessness. Image based, the only concession to language is a piece of poetry sung in falsetto by cabaret personality Ivan Davies, the *Singing Seas*.

Sister Bestial, a five-minute film, is extremely powerful in its rawness. *Sister Bestial* was originally devised as one of two films in a project titled *Chuckle Red, Chuckle Blue*. This was the gay offside to the film *Timetrap* by lesbian filmmaker, Sally Smith. The documentary style is allowed full flight. Filmed entirely in mid-shot and close-up, the hand-held camera is constantly on the move, almost another character in the stormswept forest. Images blur on this dark and windy night, lightning flashes and intense colour, reds and blue. The camera acts as an antagonist, unsettling by its presence, entering into territorial places, but where the boundaries begin and end is hard to determine.

Rachel Churchward,
Ngati Runka,
Ngati Rangi and
Ngati Kahungungu

Churchward trained with Don Selwyn at *He Taonga a Waiatarau*. The crew for this film included other students of this course. Made on the cheap, Rachel gained access to production facilities during downtime, a common and necessary practice amongst New Zealand filmmakers. Rachel sees gender issues as her primary concern.

Describing herself as 'an urban cowgirl', and a fan of country music, she wrote a script based around a relationship. *Fool For You* portrays the misunderstanding between Johnny and Peggy, a *Pakeha* couple. The questions *Fool For You* raises are: even if you live with a partner, do you ultimately know that person? Can you know what actions they will take? Set against Patsy Cline's song *Crazy*, it is easily distinguished from the music video format because of its strong narrative base, medium-paced editing and by its inclusion of action sounds in the soundtrack.

Fool For You cuts between two interiors. One is a domestic interior in which Peggy prepares dinner, pausing to ask aloud, 'Johnny, are you home?' The film shows the mundane and routine aspect of her (woman's) life. Controlled tracking shots from left to right then right to left and so on, follow Peggy's movements as she prepares the evening meal. The meal includes an extremely large fish, which introduces a macabre

note when thick blood oozes from the fish's freshly slit belly.

The shiny kitchen surfaces contrast with the space Johnny occupies. Dark and shadowy, Johnny has a gunshot wound near his temple, he lies in a pool of blood with glazed and opened eyes. The hand-held camera tempts us as it blurs uneasily over this body and past the note held in Johnny's hand. The vague space Johnny occupies represents the unknowingness that exists between him and Peggy. The film ends in slow motion on the note: 'I'm Sorry Babe, More Fool You'.

Churchward is increasingly involved in production for

Stratford Productions. Rachel has, in collaboration with its director Bruce Sheridan, made several music videos for the successful New Zealand band *The Headless Chickens*, which she manages.

Tim Worrall of Tuhoe, made *Savage Rites*, an eight-minute, 16-mm film set in 1863 that reinterprets New Zealand's history. *Savage Rites* compares the notion of myth and reality by portraying two differing viewpoints of a *Waikato* land battle with Imperial troops. Worrall re-inter-prets this tribal history to reclaim it. Intertitles inform us:

from the days when venturesome trading brigs and schooners lay at uneasy anchor in NZ bays, down to the last shot against Te Kooti in the Urewera ranges, the story of contact between European and Maori is full of episodes of the quality which makes the true romance...while each week sees the arrival of another speedy man'o'war from England or Australia carrying Imperial Troops – hardy adventurers with a glint in their eye.

A histrionic portrayal of the colonialist view is created by Worrall, using a silent film format of sepia toning, intertitles, overblown acting style and a piano accompaniment. This footage is gradually intercut with colour film representing the *Waikato* viewpoint, soundtrack is minimal, just a few real-istic bush sounds, and the acting is restrained, conveying the seriousness of a later ambush.

Merata Mita, *Ngati Pikiao* of *Te Arawa* is the most experi-enced, prolific and best-known of the directors presented here. Her work has achieved critical acclaim in New Zealand and abroad. Mita worked in the *Maori* Department of Television New Zealand but was dissatisfied with departmental boundaries, she left and went on to make several collabora-tive documentaries: *Bastion Point-Day 507*, *The Hammer and the Anvil*, *Keskidee-Aroha*, *The Bridge: A Story of Men in Dispute*. Mita directed *Karanga Hokianga*, *Patu!*, *Mauri* and *S*. Mita has faced opposition and gained sup-port from within the institutions. What is more important is the spiritual and financial support she receives from within the *Maori* community, from *kuia* and *kaumatua*, *iwi* as well as *Maori* gangs.

Mauri is a powerful feature film that evokes the quintessen-tial spiritual dimension of land and *whanau* to *Maori*. The beauty and uniqueness of our New Zealand landscape is captured in *Mauri*. A major strength in New Zealand experimental filmmaking has been its ability to evoke the land. This is evidenced in all of Mita's films, but also in many New Zealand films including *Sister Bestial* discussed earlier. The feature film

5 The Springbok Rugby Tour, 1981 was a series of tests between the New Zealand and South African Rugby Teams. Support and opposition divided New Zealand. Matches were marked by a large police presence

Mana Waka was originally commissioned by Princess Te Puea in 1937. Piecing together a narrative some fifty years later from fragments of archival footage was an important and spiritual work. Mita edited at *Turangawaewae Marae* so that elders could oversee the decisions made during post-production.

Mita's film *Bastion Point – Day 507* is a 26-minute partisan documentary covering the historic events leading up to the eviction of *Ngati Whatua* land-rights protesters. The Bastion Point occupation began in 1987, but this documentary wasn't completed until 1980. *Bastion Point – Day 507* carries the immediacy of that event today. The documentary continues to be relevant as *Maori* struggle to regain land rights and monetary compensation, using the Treaty of Waitangi as a legal and binding document. *Bastion Point* was a political consciousness raiser for *Maori* and *Pakeha* alike. It was a forerunner to the Springbok Rugby Tour of 1981[5] which Mita covered in her film *Patu*. This demonstrated to the world a country in conflict, dispelling the myth of New Zealand as a model of racial harmony.

Viewers are often shocked by *Bastion Point – Day 507*, never imagining the possibility of civil war in New Zealand. This work is powerful, often drawing emotional reactions from the audience. Mita is skilled in drawing the viewers' affinities with the protesters. A minimal use of female voiceover conveys the seriousness and power of the situation. The female voice is one not often employed in documentary films, but is used successfully. Beginning in the morning of the 507th day of occupation, the build up to confrontation is reflected in the increasing editing pace. The coverage by the local Auckland radio station's announcements brings a strong sense of immediacy. One-hundred-and-fifty, non-violent protesters are eventually dragged from the land by 600 policemen. The state pulls out all stops, the noise of the helicopters fills the soundtrack, army trucks arrive in hoards and 'scab labour' finishes the job of toppling the ramshackle huts. The voice of the state bolstered with megaphone is countered by *haka* and song.

Lisa Reihana,
Ngai Tu and Ngati Hine
of Ngaa Puhi

I have made two short works since completing my training at Elam Art School at Auckland University. *Wog Features* is a fast and furious eight-minute film using animation and live action addressing racism in culture and gender. I chose animation because of its universal appeal to children as well as adults, and to increase the potential audience. Using popular modes of music video and rap music, the film whips along unfolding a series of language-based vignettes. Sayings such as 'salt of the earth', 'a rose by any other name would smell as sweet', and 'you're getting under my skin' are portrayed visually.

Wog Features is graphic and quirky in appearance, this belies its serious undertone. The use of souvenirs is potentially contentious because they have become tourist commodities, by incorporating them into *Wog Features* I reclaim their cultural relevance. Minstrels dance in blackface; golliwogs are incorporated into reconstructions of children's television. This politicised look at culture is almost on the edge of profanity. I feel the education of our people should begin when they are young.

TAUIRA a 15-minute S-VHS video is the longest and most technically sophisticated work I have made. Three separately edited videos are sequenced by a computer to place them on a 36-monitor Videowall at Auckland's *Aotea* Centre. The grid system that the 36 monitors offer is used

▶ *Tauira*
Lisa Reihana

in a graphic way, well suited to *Maori* art-forms. *TAUIRA* incorporates *Maori* patterns that evolve from *taniko*, *whakairo*, and *tukutuku* to *kowhaiwhai*.

The main concept is travelling through a *Nui*. The *Whare Nui* is where *Maori* gather to *korero*, hold *hui* and sleep. Its architecture is constructed in such a way that it is light at the entrance which moves toward darkness. The more recent, carved ancestral figures are near the front, the earlier ancestors at the back. We move towards our ancestors, who are in front of us. *Poupou*, the ancestral carvings, are recreated using intertwined dancers. It's a surprise when they blink, to remind us that the carvings do represent real people. *TAUIRA* ends with a series of tracking shots that move from the left to the right side of screen, then from the right to the left side of screen. The actors are shown first in contemporary clothing, then in traditional clothing, again the reference of moving toward our ancestors. The soundtrack uses a nose flute during this last section to impart an eerie and ancient quality.

I use my artwork as a point of self discovery and key into my *Maori* culture. I create my own interpretations of traditional concepts and artforms in a way that I feel comfortable with, whilst still pushing the boundaries. I created a 'generic' *Whare Nui* because I know as an urban *Maori*, it could be problematic to use ancestral figures. My strategy is one of quiet subversion. By creating a contemporary *marae*, no taboos are transgressed, but issues are being dealt with. The creation of positive female images is paramount as is the use of street music, and using young actors, so that the urbanised can identify themselves within our evolving culture.

Final thoughts   I want to resist closure because a tidy ending would not reflect what is happening for *Maori* filmmaking. *Maoritanga* is not stuck in a nineteenth-century world view. Film and video is the major medium in which people now receive information, this medium has an important role to play in teaching people ways to perceive our culture. *Maori* filmmakers accept this responsibility as part of their *kaupapa*; and are constantly pushing boundaries, ideas, and ways of seeing our-

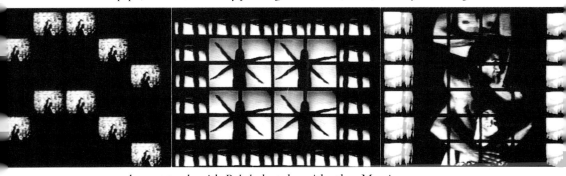

selves, not only with *Pakeha* but also with other *Maori*.

Maoritanga is being captured on the news, in documentary and drama, in short and feature films. There is a variety of subjects being tackled and motivating reasons; the effects of colonisation, different perceptions of history, the creation of archives, gender, and sexual lifestyles are being explored. The issues continue to diversify as the technical knowledge increases, and the numbers of *Maori* filmmakers throughout the industry continues to grow. *Iwi* Television, aimed specifically to a *Maori* audience, will provide an outlet that may satisfy a more traditional base such as our elders and rural communities, who should not be overlooked.

What is interesting, and often painful, is the balancing act required in reinterpreting our cultural heritage through contemporary Western traditions. Here lies the risk inherent in experimental filmmaking: not only does it stretch and reframe our way of thinking; it runs the risk of diluting the culture, our *Maoritanga* . This is the risk we take.

Glossary

Aotearoa North Island or all of New Zealand; *aroha* to love; to sympathise; *E Tipu E Rea* The murmuring noise grows; *He Taonga a Waiatarau* The treasure of Waiatarau (suburb in Auckland), A media course for *Maori* and Polynesian Students; *haka* fierce dance with chant; *hui* to gather; a meeting; *iwi* tribe; bone; people; strength; *karakia* prayer; service; *Karanga Hokianga* The Call of Hokianga (in the north of North Island); *kaumatua* old man, respected elder; *kaupapa* foundation, factors, topic, rule; *Kimihia* (to) look for; *korero* speak; news; converse; *kowhaiwhai* scroll work on rafters (of *Whare Nui*); *kuia* old lady; respected elder; *Mana Waka* Power of the Waka; *Maori* ordinary; fresh; native people; *Maoritanga* Maori culture; *marae* meeting ground, *Mauri* life principle; special character; *Ngati Whatua* Tribe of Whatua (Auckland area); *Pakeha* not *Maori*; European; *Patu* to beat, weapon. *poupou* posts; old folk; *Roimata* tears; *Tagata Pasifica* people of the Pacific; *Tainui* Tribe of central North Island; *taniko* embroidered border; *TAUIRA* example; student; tutor; draft; *Te Karere* The Messenger; *Te Kooti* Important Maori prophet and spiritual leader; *Te Manu Aute* The Bird of the Mulberry Bark; *Te Manuka* The Tea-tree; *Te Moemoea* The Dream; *Tino Rangatiratanga* The (Very) Principality; *Titiro Ngaa Pakoko* Look at the Images; *tukutuku* panel work; *Turangawaewae Marae* Waikato *Marae*; *Urewera* Central North Island; *Waikato* Tribe south of Auckland; *waka* canoe; *Waka Huia* The Treasure Box; *whakairo* carving; *whakapapa* genealogical table; cultural identity; *whare nui* big house; *whanau* family; *whenua* placenta; land; country.

The video stills are taken from VHS video copies and digitally processed onto colour laser copies. Often, this was not the originating format of the work, but was one way of obtaining the stills and getting a similar standard in print

Marian Pastor Roces

Marian Pastor Roces runs TAO Management, which develops and manages projects requiring cultural research. She was founding director of the *Museo ng Kalinangang Pilipino* (Museum of Philippine Culture), at the Cultural Center of the Philippines.

She lectured at the Humanities Department of the University of the Philippines and the Communication Arts Department of De La Salle University. Her writing over the past two decades has maintained an enquiry into the continuities and disjunctions between tradition and modernity as experienced in the Philippines.

Desert Song

A Hanging
(A Beheading?)

A Filipino was reportedly scheduled for hanging (or beheading) in Riyadh, on Christmas Day, 1992: the crime, preaching Christianity in an Islamic state. Through the newspapers, the preacher's mother broadcast a shrilly-heard appeal for Philippine President Fidel V. Ramos to urge the Saudi rulers to abort the execution. A commotion developed in Manila, with this-that-and-the-other columnist, church leader, non-governmental organisation, citizen and kibitzer throwing out strident opinions pell-mell. The preacher himself was quoted by the papers as being quite unrepentant, and indeed possessed of a martyr's zeal: hapless victim of religious fascism was he, it appeared.

Ramos (who was not provided with adequate information by his own diplomatic corps) appealed to King Fahd for clemency. After Christmas, it came to pass that the preacher was not put to death and Filipinos learned that the Saudis do not punish preaching with death (deportation is the official response to this audacity). Still, missionary endeavors are not viewed sanguinely in that country, and perhaps Ramos was wise to act with alacrity.

From the Philippine Ambassador to Saudi Arabia, a Muslim Filipino, was registered a note of protest (in kindly diplomatese) against the unreasonable panic of his Christian countrymen. Humane justice, reasoned he, does prevail in that Saudi region of the earth, the meta-message being: heavens, they are not that barbarous (or, given the Filipinos' sense of the Mideast as fabulations upon such Broadway-cum-

Hollywood inventions as *Kismet* or *The Desert Song* – an oriental's Orientalism which, because the Filipino-as-oriental is a problematic construct, misaligns the geographic orientation of the map of inequity critiqued by Said – the Ambassador might as well have cautioned: this is not an Ali Baba story!).

Ramos explained through his spokesperson that although his data lacked accuracy, he was impelled to move quickly to try and avert that horrific Christmas Day prospect – no matter the ensuing diplomatic *faux pas*. Meanwhile, the preacher's mother's faith was affirmed on the day

Pinoy preacher to be hanged in Saudi on Christmas Day
MOTHER APPEALS TO RAMOS TO INTERCEDE ON HER SON'S BEHALF
By AL PEDROCHE

celebrating the birth of Jesus in that same Mideast, by the miracle she sought in prayer and her initiation into political action. Thence appeared blissful pictures of the youthful preacher himself, alive and holding his child saved, not by his president nor his faith, but by the same cross-cultural violences which brought him very close to the final test of his sense of self.

The incident was perversely comic, however sorrowful: the scheduled hanging of a Christian preacher on Christmas Day took on the shape of parody as it bathetically plugged into the powerful martyr motifs of the great Christian stories.

Ramos appeals to King Fahd to grant clemency to RP preacher
SCHEDULED TO BE HANGED ON CHRISTMAS DAY
By BOBBY CAPO

The Filipino's self-representation as allegory of St Peter: the preacher reportedly tried to build a church. In Manila, the story also plugged into a parochial sense of international current events. Mention of Salman Rushdie was inevitable.

Yet this was by no means a Rushdie sort of tale either in the local news, the 'Rushdie affair' was signifier for Arab savagery. It was the ominous timing of the execution-which-was-not, which was viewed in the Philippines with a sense of a sacred, fatal destiny

It is this martyr motif which is the most obvious reticulation in a small universe of complexly twisted synapses growing between the Philippines and the Mideast.

A phantastic perplexity resides in the fact of a Filipino Christian preacher. The paradoxical figure from a South-east Asian island

EDITORIAL
Timely intercession and a big hear

The timely intercession of President Ramos and the big heart of King Fahd of the Kingdom of Saudi Arabia have saved from execution a Filipino preacher who is ready and willing to die for his religious beliefs.

Oswaldo "Wally" Magdangal was

last Dec. 22 Magdangal's impend doom based on the exclusive interview his mother by our Malacanang repor Al Pedroche, providentially a born-ag Christian.

We are happy that President Ram acted with dispatch and succeeded in

who believes himself heir to and vessel of a Middle-Eastern religion, through the auspices of European conquest, and thenceforth returning the religion, to the desert, provides the story with a pall of utter futility. The forces coursing through the person of the preacher are conceivable in. terms of an almost geologic time, or a curlicuing, Sherazad-esque (Arabesquing!) time.

By some hideous symmetry, the preacher's multiple annihilations seem so involved in renaissances. His intensified faith, for instance, issued from the Christian fundamentalism which sprung out of Reagan's America and swept through the Philippines at just about that most curious moment when Filipinos were reassessing the American presence in their islands. More, this born-again passion, with its middle-class character, gains clarity as cultural expression when juxtaposed with the upper-class fervor for religious-economic-political power configurations; the standard neocolonialism. It is germane to add that in the Philippines, the Spain-originated *Opus Dei* has been exercising a truly tight grip on high government office, from the end of the Marcos period through most of the Aquino period, to today. And to the Latinate economics of this ruling priesthood might be traced the source of one agency driving hundreds of thousands of middle-class Filipinos to seek jobs in other lands.

But then again, to take the long view that purports to encompass, the entire colonial period and then some, has the effect of reducing the human condition to an archeological dig. Political activism in this site is merely a wailing wall, not much more than a space for lamentation. The plight of the Filipino labourer in the Mideast is rendered bloodless by attempts to promote the breadth of scholarship, as indeed an archeological site is completly non-sensuous: there is no recoil from the remnants of faeces, vomits, foods, struggles, and can be handled with an austere distance.

Vanishings in the desert   Activism, of course, can only lock tenaciously onto the existential present. Each threatened or extinguished human life is necessarily a focus, and each of these one-thousand-and-one foci have to be enveloped in a compelling now-ness: not for the activist is the aesthete's, or the scholar's, archeology.

Here, for instance, is a petition:

With conviction, the KANLUNGAN[1] CENTER FOUNDATION, INC. wholeheartedly supports the attached petition of OCW [Overseas Contract Workers] families to resolve the cases of deaths and disappearance of their loved ones. In sympathy and compassion, we join the bereaved families in seeking justice for:

GLENDA ALLAMADO , who alledgedly committed suicide in ABU DHABI, UNITED ARAB EMIRATES, by jumping from the 6th floor of the building where she resided. GLENDA'S REMAINS HAVE YET TO BE REPATRIATED .

REBECCA DIMACULANGAN, who succumbed to death in the UNITED ARAB EMIRATES under harrowing and unthinkable circumstances. Autopsy reports indicate she was raped and died of strangulation by hand.

MARGIE MILTANTE, who went to work in RIYADH, SAUDI ARABIA in a healthy physical and mental condition but was reported to have died of cardio-vascular arrest due to a latent disease. The NBI [Philippines' National Bureau of Investigation] autopsy report however avers that Margie died of pneumonia.[2]

VILMA SADARAN, whose death in BAHRAIN was marred by untold misery. The NBI autopsy report includes laceration of private parts, bruises and bumps or fractures in the skull.[3]

JOHMAR ANTONIO who, one day in September 1990 mysteriously disappeared in SAUDI ARABIA. Two years of enquiries yielded no meaningful response from the Department of Foreign Affairs, the Philippine Overseas Employment Administration and/or other government agencies.

Severed ligaments and fragments of sundered minds are folded into text, as each tragedy is reified and represented via the form of petition or manifesto. In the Philippines, this is most effective, and perhaps differently so from the careers of similar modes of textualisation used in political struggle elsewhere. The immediacy – the representation of a large-scale violence as a name, or a face, or a story of an individual crisis – works on the enormous reservoir of guilt of the Christian majority (and sometimes plays crudely on the outrage of the Muslim minority, as when a news report

1 *Kanlungan* is a Tagalog word referring to a sheltering roof, shed or space

2 While this essay was being prepared, a news item reported that Margie Militante died in Riyadh, Saudi Arabia, 21 May 1992, because of 'cardiovascular arrest due to latent disease'. The report made no mention of the stab wound in the stomach, the broken left arm and the contusions in several parts of her body, which her family noted upon the arrival in the Philippines of Militante's remains, frozen, naked and wrapped only in a blanket

3 In the same report, it was written that Vilma Sadaran's death was caused by 'asphyxia by hanging', as reported by Bahraini officials

4 The petition is signed by Mary Lou L. Alcio, Chairperson, Board of Trustees, and Gina Alunan-Melgar, Executive Director of Kanlungan Center Foundation, Inc. a Center for Migrant Workers holding offices at 77-K 10th cor. KJ Sts., Kamias, Quezon City, Philippines

stated that 'even Muslim Filipinos are abused'). It also works on a sacral sense of family and small community, as indeed families and communities are extrapolated by a great many Filipinos to mean 'the Philippines'. The petition above ends thus:

*Indeed, cases of abuse and maltreatment to Filipino overseas workers are increasing and a number has resulted to [sic] eventual, untimely deaths, mysterious disappearances and/or insanities. The families of the above victims are but a few who are emboldened to seek speedy resolution and justice for their loved ones – as they have not, at this time, lost their faith and confidence in the government. As it must be noted that a number who have been victimised in the overseas employment have and/or are opting to merely heal their wounded heart in silence – either due to lost [sic] of confidence or feeling of utter hopelessness. Again and on this occasion, we ask the concerned officials and the concerned agencies, **What is happening to our 'new heroes'?** – the overseas workers, who in their collective effort have contributed so much to resuscitate our economy.*[4]

Like Ramos's reponse to the reported hanging, those whose mission it is to help the troubled overseas worker do necessarily act in the context of urgencies and small units of stories, as though one family were appealing to another – and shall we set aside, for the moment, how we all got into the scrape in the first place. (An impatience: we all know how we got here. We need the money. We got underfoot of the World Bank-IMF, the Americans, the Spaniards, and let's not forget the Japanese.)

Invoking the familial – and reinventing the Filipino family as it stretches its fragile definitions and connections across the globe – seems to be the consistent reaction to the incomprehensible weight of each cross-cultural crisis situation. Overseas-contract workers from the Philippines, as do other Others, do need to be able to retreat into whatever is left to them of some kind of sacred ground. But for the Filipino who is, precisely, an overseas-contract worker – a person who migrates to work for a specific duration and expects to return home – home, in howevei a vanished form, can and does remain the location of wholeness. This is probably not the case with migrants who cut themselves off completely from the notion of return.

Much of the political activity surrounding the issue of overseas workers is targetted towards appealing to or critiquing the Philippine government or some of its officials, rather than towards international lob-

144 domes

One hundred and forty-four
Filipina overseas domestic workers were repatriated from Kuwait yesterday, most of them
complaining of maltreatment and
sexual harassment by employers.

They said their Kuwaiti employers gave them unjust wages,
inadequate food and poor accom-
modation, made them work until
early morning, and the others
were subjected to sexual abuse or
harassment.

They also said their employers brought them to the police
stations and not to hospitals when
they get sick.

Even Muslim Filipina wor **Re**

bying. Although an increasing number of non-government organisations are beginning to put up refuge centres in the countries where Filipino labourers have flocked, it is still largely expected that the Philippine government, or individual senators, congressmen, local government leaders – like village elders or heads of families – undertake the work of negotiating with foreign employers and their governments. Government is therefore carefully watched. Officials/'elders' are required to behave with the compassion of relatives in authority roles.

The grotesqueries encountered in the Middle East are expected. The island-born villager's family sells the carabao, the year's crop, the parcel of land, to pay off a labyrinthine hierarchy of corrupt officials and ghoulish recruiters for the prize of a short-term contract to be a welder, mechanic, carpenter, nurse, domestic helper, driver, pipe-fitter in Abu Dhabi, Bahrain, Qatar, Kuwait, Iran, Iraq, Saudi Arabia (and even Rejkjavik, and recently there was talk of Siberia and Vladivostok): furthermore, this person fully expects to come close to moments where the dangers include beheading, imprisonment, rape, torture, virtual slavery, or getting stranded in the middle of wars. This person is, for now, incapable of blaming foreign employers for their torments. The joke which always gets the laugh: a Filipino who gets run over by a speeding Mercedes with an Arab driver in Saudi Arabia is at fault – for being there.

This person will try to escape certain types of torture, try a slave's appeal to the foreign master, on occasion kill the master, try to send word back to their families, try to test the limits of their toughness and guile, indeed try a few entertaining subversions like getting drunk where it is forbidden. (Theft and gambling, among other petty crimes, are rife among Filipinos in the Middle East.)

What cannot be countenanced is a lack of compassion from the archipelagic homeland. The relocated/dislocated labourers and their relatives will work themselves into an incantatory roaring when it strikes them that their Filipino 'parents', 'godparents', 'elders' in government have abandoned them to their doom. At the moment, there is enough forbearance towards a government which is selling the entire labour force of the Philippines to foreign markets like a pimp out of, among other powerlessnesses, a lack of the political vigour to negotiate the country out of the debt bind. But a row is expected in Manila should anyone in the

Remains of Pinoy

... Workers

By GINA TABONARES

assistance to investigate the
circumstances surrounding
their relatives' mysterious
deaths.

Official reports reaching
OWWA said Militante died in
Riyadh, Saudi Arabia last May
21 because of "cardiovascular
arrest due to latent disease."

OWWA also said that Sada-
ran's death was "asphyxia by
hanging" as reported to them
by officials of Bahrain.

Corpin said he had in-
structed the OWWA officers
on site to assist Philippine
Embassy officials in the investigation of these cases.

The Department of Foreign
Affairs (DFA) had ...

immediately look into the
circumstances and causes of
the OCWs' deaths.

According to Abu Dhabi-
based welfare officer Musta-
pha Glang, he asked Llamado's
employer, Ismael Kheder Al-
Hosani, to shoulder the cost of
repatriation but he refused.

Glang said Llamado left her
Palestinian employer four
months before her death and

"One day,
reason, she jum
floor of the buil
and her boyfrie
Filipinos were
reported to C

Glang adde
boyfriend is r
custody whil
who were al
released and
custody of th

Masyos na Kapaligiran,
Mahusay na
Paglilingkod-Bayan

Filipino worker mi

KUWAIT -- Two Asian workers have disappeared
from the Kuwaiti side of the demilitarized border
zone and are feared held by the Iraqis, diplomats
reported Tuesday.

Gul Azim Khan, a Pakistani, and Nicanor Fac-
torin, a 48-year-old Filipino, have been missing
since Thursday.

"We have strong reasons to believe they've

been abducted
Philippine Con
Press.

The demi
year's Gulf w
occupation c
southern Ira

HOME AT LAST

Guial, 39, shields her seven-day-old baby fr
tly after arrival from Kuwait. Guial and 30 o
tic helpers were repatriated home by OWWA.

Department of Foreign Affairs or the office overseeing overseas workers so
much as utters an unkind word about the labourers abroad. For to be severed from familial kindnesses is verily the meaning of doom.

Bondings on shifting borders

Here is a newfangled family, described by the *Philippine
Daily Inquirer* in 'Yank, Pinoy recall Iraqi prison ordeal', a
sort of postscript to the recent Gulf War:

*KUWAIT – An American demolition expert and a Filipino computer specialist,
held for one month in Iraq as suspected saboteurs, said ... they were kept awake at
night by the screams of Iraqi prisoners being beaten up.
The men, who were forced to lie naked and blindfolded on concrete floors, said
they would not have survived another month of their harrowing ordeal and
would certainly have died if they had not been able to huddle together for
warmth. A third man captured on December 3 when the group ran into an Iraqi*

guard on the badly marked border – US engineer Jim Aduddell – has returned home for kidney problems and severe bruising.

'If we'd been there another month that would have been it – if we'd been separated I don't think we would have lasted', American David Martin told reporters on his return to Kuwait.

The Filipino computer engineer who huddled close to the American for life is the same man who sued the Philippine Secretary of Foreign Affairs for negligence. He might be seen as Philippine animists used to see the human being: possessed of several souls to the left and right of the body, each an active agent and seeking missing coaslescing-into states of equilibrium, from moment to moment, expecting to come together in death.

     This soul shares a lot with the legion others who fly with bravado to the desert to be able to fly home bringing gifts of casette recorders and Betamax units and 22-carat gold trinkets. And the scar tissues of valour. They fully intend to invest the few thousand dollars they bring home, in jeepneys and tricycles for ferrying – and in tiny stores selling gum and vinegar and local spirits to neighbour and co-villager. Many a survivor is able to build houses of cement to replace their parents' shanties and nipa huts, which always flew in the winds of the yearly typhoons.

Pinoy . . .

(From page 1)

American business associates David Martin and Jim Aduddell on Dec. 6, 1991, on suspicion that they were spies. They were released Jan. 4.

The three were then surveying an area along the Kuwaiti-Iraqi border for a mine-clearing project.

"(These) public officials failed to discharge their duties and functions due to their gross inexcusable negligence and inefficiency," Ducat said in an affidavit, copies of which he provided mediamen in a news conference. He is set to file criminal and administrative complaints against the three officials today.

Ducat said no Philippine embassy official or representative was sent to assist him after he was arrested and even during his trial.

He said he owed his [ ] to Polish officials who [ ] for the release of his two American friends.

Ducat's father Ventu[ ] Manglapus had not act[ ] his request that the Cat[ ] official help in getting [ ] out of jail.

Ducat said he was [ ] complaint because he [ ] want other Filipinos t[ ] his fate.

"I was lucky to b[ ] Americans. What wo[ ] happen to others? Th[ ] have rot in jail," he [ ]

Ducat said he he[ ] during his imprison[ ] another Filipina wa[ ] three months in Iraq[ ] height of the Gulf war. No embassy official had helped her, he noted.

---

8   TUESDAY, AUGUST 18, 1992

'POTENTIAL THREAT'
Migrant workers want OWW

A MIGRANT workers' group [ ] sought the recall of the [ ] head of the

his shares in the family-owned DPC Placement and Manpower Services.

[ ]'s divestment of his [ ]

overseas workers."

The group said that Cor[ ] placement firm is facing 23 [ ] before the Philippine Ov[ ] Employment Administratio[ ] recruitment violations agai[ ] The cases involve[ ] [ ]ages, [ ] dismissa[ ] [ ]e docume[ ] [ ]ck recor[ ] [ ]stry, he [ ] [ ]seas work[ ] [ ]ell as a[ ]

Pinoy detained in Iraq files suit vs Manglapus

By CHRISTINE AVENDAÑO

FOREIGN Secretary Raul Manglapus and two ambassadors based in the Middle East are facing charges before the ombudsman for allegedly neglecting the plight of a computer engineer captured by Iraqi soldiers at the border of Kuwait and Iraq last year.

Joseph Ducat, executive vice president of Ducat

Development Inc., told reporters he was filing the charges against Manglapus, Ambassador to Iraq Akmad Sakkam and Ambassador to Kuwait Mauyag Tamano, who he said ignored pleas made by his family to work for his release.

Iraqi soldiers captured Ducat along with his two
See PINOY, P. 12

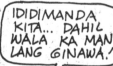

They hang up signs on vehicle or home proclaiming *Katas ng Saudi* (juice of Saudi), or *Pawis ng Saudi* (Saudi sweat), or *Katas ng langis* (oil juice), or *Katas ng buhangin* (juice from sand). In the declarations in this semiotic field, bodily juices water, fertilise, materialise treasures from out of the aridity. Indeed bodies are given, as the computer engineer needed to. The souls also speak, furtively this time, or giddily, of Arab men who wear no underpants under the flowing robes; of discovering a new, perturbing sexuality in being a nicely-brown, relatively hairless, fragile-boned male in a landscape of hirsute giants; of realising, as a substantial number of female virtual-slaves from the Philippines have, a power to kill despotic masters.

But other souls are drawn to travel, to adventuring in other people's wars and with other people's technologies to learning skills that are absolutely useless in the village back home. They live out the reconnections of their nervous systems to computers and satellites. They learn to use an international banking system, though they never so much as needed a bank where they lived their youth (and though their other souls will not be stopped from sending moneyorders to children and wives and husbands who await this grace, monthly, conveyed through the ether). They actually enjoy this astral mobility.

And having coupled with strangers, they have been recreated. Bondings on shifting borders are more than a useful metaphor. It was reported that the computer engineer was saved through the intercession of the Polish government. The silence of his Foreign Affairs Secretary through his trial is the source of his rage. It is uncertain whether the Philippine government could have done anything about the suspicion that he was implicated in espionage. It is uncertain whether the very same 'Yank' with whom he shared his body was precisely the reason for his coming to grief, or whether it was he who brought perdition to the American. But whatever the flesh of this story, the computer engineer will obviously feel less comfortable with the word Filipino.

Filipino has at best been a tentative signifier for wholeness, though the word has served the purpose of providing natives with a citizenship, useful in a world of nations. When a motley assortment of head-hunters and Muslims with sultans, and animists whose new word for Christian church is their old word for ephemeral 'shrine' (*sambahan/simbahan*), and coloniser-infatuated denizens of Spanish-built towns, were sold by Spain to the United States before the last *fin de siecle*, there was a nation only in the sense that a map with borders formalised the ownership to this piece of watery real estate. Even today, the Philippine Revolution of 1898 is considered by other ethnolinguistic groups in the archipelago to have been essentially a *Tagalog* event.

OCWs affected by Gulf war can now file their claims

By GINA TABONARES

All overseas contract work-ers (OCWs) in eastern Saudi Arabia who were affected dur- day by lawyer Venus Bravo, chief of the OWWA's legal division, who said that the

A cautionary word is being sounded in cultural studies with regard to 'ethnic absolutism'. And surely it strains the imagination to still fool around with the early-ethnographer yearning for untouched societies; and to imagine that, for instance, the overseas contract worker from a not-quite-nation such as the Philippines, should have a sense of self any more crystallised than the shifting patterns in a kaleidoscope.

There must be an 'ethnicity' there somewhere. There must be such a creature, an island Southeast Asian, they with the brown skin described in the *Tagalog* term of endearment *kayumanggi*, a word which alludes to wood, or bark. Their ancestors were similarly given to female shamanism and male warrior priesthoods. It is known that these ancestors commuted between forests and rivers which provided the orientations for shifting farms. They were naked but for tattoos, tassels, g-strings and poi-soned arrows. They ate tubers and rice, as do their progeny. They also had this prediliction for taking to the waters in boats that were lashed together, which they would occasionally dismantle for storage.

The ancestors survive in a tenacious reverence for the word for 'ancestor' (*apo*), which is also, in many Philippine languages, 'grand-children', 'progeny'. If one considers that peoples in large chunks of island Southeast Asia managed to elude the total experience of central authority, monotheism, political hegemony, even during, and certainly after, the var-ious colonisations – there might be a not too far-fetched insight here as to why an astonishing number of people from a purportedly modern country still behave like a brood given to supplicating mother-father-*apo*.

It might even be said that the travel motif that runs through the overseas contract-worker experience is nothing new. There are Austronesian speakers in Madagascar and Easter Island. Perhaps this is not fantasia: peoples whose ancestors were not daunted by the Pacific Ocean 20,000 years ago may not be all that scared of crossing over to the desert. Certainly Filipinos are in Somalia this very minute, for who-knows-what business. It may not be the travel, in fact, that is the location of today's

● Sen. Ernesto Herrera urged the Senate committee on labor employment and human resources development yesterday to investigate the mysterious deaths and dis-appearances of some Filipino contract workers in Mid-dle East and recommended appropriate legislative measures for their further protection.

anguish. There is no horror in the necessity of huddling close to another human body, no matter the skin of another colour and texture. For Filipinos who regularly sleep on mats with 6, 12, relatives of all sizes – and who can fuck with discretion too – will not be finicky about sharing warmth.

Neither should disrupted relationships be too much of a psychic strain to peoples whose patience with earthquakes and typhoons must be virtually genetic. Their geology changes before their eyes. Their families have houses perched near craters of erupting volcanos. Their seasons do not elegantly divide the almanac. Their gods (even the Christian and Islamic) have a tendency of appearing outside churches and mosques, indeed in jeepneys right next to the *Katas ng Saudi* sticker: They, too, move. Now the Philippine landscape of signs includes the Mideastern words *El Shaddai*, centre of gravity for incredible convocations of fundamentalist Catholics whose faith in 'charismatic' possibility has somehow drawn them to addressing their god in the name of the Old Testament's Hebrew rendering of 'God the Provider'. Not only disrupted, but permeable borders.

Jorma Puranen

Imaginary Homecoming

Jorma Puranen was born in 1951 and lives and works in Helsinki, Finland. where he studied photography at the University of Industrial Arts. He worked as a teacher at the University of Industrial Arts and from 1993 at the University of Gothenburg in Sweden. His work has been widely exhibited internationally since 1979. Some group and solo shows include: *Nordic Night-Nordic Light*, Asahi Pentax Gallery, Tokyo (1985), *Utopia and Memory*, Houston Fotofest, *Questioning Europe*, Galerie Krivy, Nice (1991), *Wasteland*, Rotterdam Photography Biennale (1992), Gallery Index, Stockholm (1993).

This work has its origin in many sources: in the history of photography and anthropology. But most of all it was born of long conversations with Sámi people (Lapps) about their land and history. The Sámi people are a now minority of about 50,000 - 60,000 inhabitants, living in the northern-most areas of Finland, Sweden, Norway and Russia.

Photography and anthropology share a common history. They were both innocent enough to get abused in colonial processes. With this work I wanted to prompt questions, for example, about how and with whose gaze we look at and photograph the world beyond our own culture.

Drawn from the picture archives of ethnological and anthropological museums, the oldest pictures were taken by an expedition led by Prince Roland Bonaparte in 1882; I found the collection here in the *Musée de L'Homme* in Paris. While researching archive materials of the Sámi peoples' life and culture I found portraits of mothers, fathers, grandmothers and other relatives of Sámi families that I know personally.

One of the themes of this work is an imaginary homecoming. The highlands of Upper Lapland have been the territory of nomad Sámi people. Still today they are wandering with their reindeer herds from winter pastures to the seaside for summer. I printed old portrait photographs onto Plexiglas sheets and re-photographed them on the exposed fell slopes of northern Norway and Sweden. The idea was to metaphorically return people who had been buried in archives back to the landscape and culture from which they had been separated.

◀ Installation view at
Rotterdam Biennale, 1992

Perspex and silver gelatin
prints, 1990-91,

Desperately Seeking the Dalai Lama

Clare Harris

Clare Harris is a Research Fellow in the Department of Art and Archaeology at the School of Oriental and African Studies, London University. She has a first class honours degree from Cambridge University in European Art History. She has worked as a writer and editor for the print media and in television. Her doctoral thesis analyses the evolution of Tibetan painting over the last fifty years.

In 1988 an unsuspecting Westerner was arrested in the Tibetan capital Lhasa. The story of this 'innocent abroad' made international news but his crime was neither incitation to riot nor theft of official secrets, or even of straying into delimited territory. The offence: sporting a Phil Silvers T-shirt without due care and attention. The felon had failed to notice the striking resemblance between the image of Phil Silvers, an American comic of the 1950s, and the Dalai Lama, an incarnation of the god of compassion, Nobel Peace Prize winner, exiled spiritual and political leader of the Tibetans, and therefore Public Enemy Number One as far as the Chinese authorities in Tibet are concerned. Just as it is a crime to display the Tibetan flag in Tibet, it can be dangerous to exhibit the Dalai Lama's portrait (though travel guides encourage visitors to take a wad of photographs of His Holiness to present to native Tibetans). Many foreign visitors report continuing adoration of the Dalai Lama icon, recipients of postcards, snap-shots and even newspaper cuttings break down in tears as they crush his image to their foreheads in the traditional gesture of respect. Despite Draconian attempts at cultural control, the image remains a cultural currency which has yet to be devalued. Within the refugee 'black market' this coinage moves across borders, and is reinvented by contemporary artists.

Tibet became a Buddhist nation during the reign of King Song-tsen Gampo in the seventh century. By 1950 religion had become such a vital feature of the social and cultural infrastructure of the country that some 6,000 monasteries had been built which were populated by 600,000 monks. In a land two-thirds the size of India, but far less densely populated, virtually every town and village had a religious establishment and some, such as the eastern community of Sakya, it is said to have had more than one hundred. It was therefore not surprising that when a Chinese regime with a ruthlessly materialistic ideology decided to take control of Tibet in the late 1940s one of their primary aims was to obliterate any manifestation of religion. They recognised that the image of the Dalai Lama, or any emanation of the Buddha, had symbolic connotations beyond the strictly doctrinal, and so a policy of cultural devastation was implemented. Teams of Chinese workers set about the systematic destruction of the monasteries. Sculpture made of gold, silver, brass and other metalwork inlaid with precious stones was sold either on the international art market or melted down and used to earn foreign currency. Paintings and sculpture in less lucrative materials were smashed and burnt whilst sacred *mani* stones were used to make latrine walls. Tibetans were often forced to take part in this process, or at least to watch, as slaughterhouses were set up in monasteries and the Jokhang (equivalent to a cathedral) in Lhasa was converted into a pigsty. By 1979 most of the monks and nuns were either dead, had disappeared or were hopelessly traumatised by torture.

▲ Tharpa Cholingam, *Water of Life, Bathing Figures*

Those artists who survived the cultural purge were forced to abandon traditional *thangka* (a sort of scroll painting) techniques, styles and subject matter to pursue the Socialist Realism of the post-invasion regime. According to one artist who worked in Tibet in the Cultural Revolutionary period, artists were commandeered to mass produce portraits of Chairman Mao which would replace the Buddhist images that had previously been found in every Tibetan home. Canvases depicting the heroic deeds of the People's Liberation Army as they ousted what is known as the 'Dalai Clique' were also commissioned. My informant suspects that the authorities expected artists to exorcise the spirit of Buddhism as they painted such subjects, but for many the process was so unbearable that they fled the country. Once the Dalai Lama had departed (the possibility of a kidnapping or murder attempt seemed increasingly likely in 1959) many Tibetans also decided to escape cultural and religious intolerance and became part of the first wave of refugees, now well over 100,000 world-wide. Several of the most illustrious painters made the journey into India carrying with them as many drawings, paintings and notes as they could in an attempt to reclaim something from the wasteland that Tibet had become, and became crucial to the process of re-establishing a culture over the border.

But perhaps the most valuable commodity that the painters brought with them was memory. Once in exile the Amdo artist Jamyang Losal recounted the iconometric and iconographic details of over two hundred deities and published them in *The New Sun Self Learning Book on the Art of Tibetan Painting* for the benefit of those who would have no concept of life as it had been lived in Tibet before Chinese control. He also decorated the walls of the Tibetan temple at Mussoorie in Uttar Pradesh (India) entirely according to a design which he remembered from the homeland.

Once the refugees had survived the initial hardships of the tented camps and years of labouring on road building projects in the Himalayas, they began to establish more stable communities, and to devote some of their funds to the formation of monasteries and a revival of the traditional arts. The centre for most of this activity was, and remains, the so-called 'capital in exile' at Dharamasala in Himachal Pradesh. The Dalai Lama was particularly keen to encourage painters, musicians, performers, writers and craftsmen to record what they had learnt in Tibet and to pass this on to the generations born in exile. He commissioned *thangkas* for use in his own meditational practice and set artists to work on wall paintings in the new religious buildings and studios where they could teach others. The most important of the early exiled artists was Jampa Tseten (born 1928 – died 1988?) who had been a Senior State Artist in Tibet. He was later followed by Rigzin Peljor (born 1933 – died 1991) a Junior State Artist from a family with a long lineage of master painters. The monk painter Sangay Yeshi has also enjoyed the support of His Holiness and still runs a school in Dharamasala training young artists in *thangka* techniques. Those refugee artists who are most closely tied to the religious and political establishment of the exiled culture are primarily involved in a nostalgic recreation of *temps perdus*; an inevitable process of conscious archaism which could easily lead to the ossification of Tibetan art. Repetition, veering towards out-and-out copying has been a feature of *thangka* painting for some time, as Hugh Richardson and David Snellgrove noted when discussing art of the eighteenth century in *The Cultural History of Tibet*. A certain sterility is now apparent in Tibetan crafts, art-forms, literature, imagery and all the rest.

But the question arises: what now becomes of Tibetan civilisation? Does it continue to flourish always in the same stereotyped forms, contrary to all we observe elsewhere in the history of civilisations? It is almost a general rule that when any culture becomes cut off from outside influences and ceases to develop new forms, it is already moribund?

When discussing twentieth-century developments the two historians fail to comment on the impact of just those 'outside influences' whose omission they lament. Along with the anthropologist Christoph von Furer-Haimendorf they merely skate over the matter of the new conditions with references to 'living traditions'. Furer-Haimendorf states:

Under the inspiring leadership of their traditional ruler and spiritual head, His Holiness the Dalai Lama, Tibetans of all classes who had succeeded in escaping from the Chinese grip set about reconstructing the culture which had unfolded over centuries in Tibet, and aroused the admiration of all those aware of its aesthetic and spiritual uniqueness.

But this sort of vision oversimplifies the story and places the Dalai Lama, as embodiment of the culture, on a life-support machine for perpetuity. The tourism which now engulfs the capital in exile (Dharamasala) threatens to make him the Mickey Mouse to the Tibetan Disneyland. For outsiders whose only experience of Tibet will be through the refugee communities the culture can have the atmosphere of a mock-up. This has a great deal to do with the fact that, as they will admit, some Tibetans have deliberately played up to the West's *idée fixe* since they know enough about the way in which the West acquires its information to play the game.

The Shangri-La vision of Tibet, which still holds sway in many quarters in the West, insists on an idealisation of the Tibetans as ethereal and other-worldly, the repositories of a secret knowledge no longer available to the rest of the earth's population.

Even anecdotal evidence about the 13th Dalai Lama contradicts the thesis. As a small boy he was known to have loved mechanical things and been intrigued by a pedal car presented to him by the British. Fortunately there have been other Tibetans with a similar fascination for novelty and sophistication, and there is a strand of rebellion amongst the Tibetan creative community which may help to prevent the culture from becoming deep-frozen in response to the idealisation of outsiders or of reactionary tendencies within.

Even before the exodus of the early 1960s some exceptional Tibetans had gained exposure to the outside world and begun to produce images and texts of a revolutionary nature by Tibetan standards. Gedun Chompel was one such man. Born in 1905 he visited India and explored a brave new world of politics, literature and art, producing a translation of the *Kama Sutra* in Tibetan and drawings which were influenced by modern

▶ Sakya Dagchen Jigdal Rinpoche, husband of Jamyang Sakya, on his motorcycle in Lhasa, 1957

Indian and European art. However he gained notoriety for his radical views and on his return to Tibet found himself in jail. His suicide in 1951 indicates the severity of the strain he experienced when trying to experiment with new ideas in Tibet. But there were others. At Tharpa Choling in Darjeeling, West Bengal, a Tibetan monastery established outside the home country in the 1940s, there are wall paintings following traditional themes which show the direct impact of photographic imagery from the Second World War. In the segment of the *Wheel of Life* which for centuries has been used to depict the battle of the titans or demi-gods against the gods in their blissful realm, the artist paints the warriors in ancient Tibetan battle dress but he also introduces early aircraft, howitzers and the uniforms of twentieth century warfare in a montage which employs the style of news pictures and cartoons to demonstrate the relevance of Buddhist philosophy in the modern world. The demi-gods were doomed to be reborn to fight eternal battles in this section of the Karmic cycle because they had envied the power of the gods in a previous life. In the Tibetan scheme of things Hitler and Mussolini would be justly consigned to this kind of purgatory.

Evidence that Tibetans inside Tibet were also not utterly isolated from the cultural and scientific developments which transformed Europe in the late nineteenth and early twentieth centuries is available.

The prevalent Western preconception of Tibetans as non-materialistic, spiritual beings with little regard for the vanities of the physical world is exploded by photographs such as the portrait of the monk Sakya Dugchen Rinpoche taken in 1957. Clad in full monastic robes he sits astride his motorcycle in front of a painted studio backdrop of distinctly Chinese character as though he had just driven out to the pagoda by the lake for a picnic. The formal arrangement of this type of portraiture is not dissimilar from that found in India and China in the 1930s and 1940s, though it was probably only available to the aristocratic families of Lhasa. Portraits of important religious figures, with or without motorcycles, must have begun to circulate in wealthy circles before the upheavals of 1959, since they found their way to India with the refugees. Amongst some of the first paintings to be produced in exile were collages in which a photograph has been incorporated into an otherwise traditionally painted composition, such as *Photorealism Thangka; Ladakh*. This technique will come as a surprise to those who have learnt of the iconometric system which is repeatedly said to have dominated Tibetan art.

The artistic canon does include some texts with strict regulations for the depiction of divine and not-so-divine figures. These specify measurements and grids for use when painting everything, in theory, from the Buddha to a milkman (though portraits of secular figures are rare) and deviation from these rules was a risky business. Both the producer and viewer of an ill-formed *thangka* risked personal misfortune, in fact such errors might 'lead one to hell' as the painter Pema Namdol Thaye comments in his *Concise Tibetan Art Book*:

The image must be accurate. An erroneous image cannot be blessed and consecrated. Such images should be in remote and deserted places as they are more harm than benefit to Human society.

But whilst Tibetan art has an elaborate system of codification for producing icons worthy of use in religious practice, it also presents a strong vein of interest in realism. Jamyang Losal, who left Tibet in the early 1960s seeking asylum in India 'following Chinese aggression on my country', relates the tale of one of his predecessors.

Once an artist painted a beautiful flower and a man, on seeing it, complimented him on its beauty. He wanted to grow that flower and so asked for its seed. The painter said, 'If you like this flower, then take it home.' The man felt happy and began to pick up the flower only to realise that it was not real. He felt ashamed.... It is amazing that even in those days something akin to modern art existed.

Accounts of the miraculous veracity of certain images are common in the writings of both artists and commentators, but it is significant that Jamyang equates realism with modernity. He is pinpointing an increasing trend away from the formality of Tibetan style towards a sort of super-realism and of course if it's verisimilitude you're after, then the camera is the ideal tool. A major impetus towards the development of the life-like portrait during the Italian Renaissance was said to have been the demand from patrons for accurate portrayals of friends or mentors to be preserved after their death. It could be said that every commission which a contemporary Tibetan refugee artist completes stems from a similar motive; to preserve not just the memory of an individual but of an entire culture which has gone, never to return.

▲ The Dalai Lama

Many Tibetans and their supporters hope that the final death toll has yet to be struck, and hope for a return to the homeland and a revivification of the culture on the person of the Dalai Lama. Despite the enormous reverence with which he is approached by most Tibetans, the monkish media star has inspired new ideas and images.

In the corner of the home of a Tibetan refugee a framed poster of His Holiness has been displayed with a white *kathak* or scarf of blessing. The poster is a copy of a 'modern' *thangka* in which the beatific vision of the Dalai Lama, eyes closed as if in meditation (and wearing the 1950s style glasses which led to the Phil Silvers confusion) is taken from a photograph. The artist appears to have decided that the truthfulness of the mechanically produced image can be readily incorporated amongst Tibetan aesthetic precepts. Where the iconometric system traditionally ensured that the power of the image was not damaging to artist or viewer, the camera has taken over. All other features of this composition, the Dalai Lama's throne, robes and tables decorated with symbolic offerings are portrayed in the classic Tibetan manner with a high degree of emphasis on pattern and flattened surfaces contrasting with the three dimensionality of the photographic face.

Though apparently contradictory on an aesthetic level this combination makes sense, since in philosophic terms the only 'real' ele-

ment is the person, and specifically the mind of the Dalai Lama. Everything
else is simply a reflection of the Buddha of Compassion. Since the Dalai
Lama as a man makes the principle of compassion active in the real world,
his physical characteristics are the supreme expression of that principle.
The three *thangkas* hanging on the wall behind his throne and framing his
head all represent facets of the Dalai Lama's spiritual 'personality':
Kalachakra (the Wheel of Time) on the left, the four-armed manifestation
of *Chenrezig*, (the Bodhisatva of Compassion) on the right and *Sakyamuni*
(the Prince Siddhartha who became the living Buddha) in the centre. The
present Dalai Lama seems to have a special affinity with the concepts which
both the text and visual representation of Kalachakra embody and he frequently gives teachings based on it. Chenrezig, can be seen as the idealised
portrayal of the Dalai Lama's nature and Sakyamuni the fundamental principle behind it. On top of these levels of meaning the devotee to whom this
thangka belongs has customised it with his own photographs and a postcard
of another Kalachakra *thangka*. The combination of the continuing
potency of the Dalai Lama icon and the impact of new techniques, materials and conditions has inspired a reinvention of tradition.

      Whilst the character of the exiled artistic community has
been described here primarily in terms of conscious archaisms there are
those who are looking to the future. Pema Namdol Thaye, a twenty-some-
thing painter now based in Kalimpong, West Bengal is highly innovative in
Tibetan terms. At the age of twenty-one he published The *Concise Tibetan
Art Book* and has created wall paintings and *thangkas* for patrons in India
and the broader Tibetan Diaspora. Pema inherited a fusion of two great
Tibetan painting styles (Menri and Karma Gadri) from his uncle, a master
painter trained in Tibet, but brings a verve to it which is entirely his own.
When it comes to interpretation of the *Jatakas*, (texts in which the life of
the Buddha is recorded) which he explores in the murals of Zangdrak Palri
monastery just outside Kalimpong, he reflects the environment in which he
grew up. His depiction of the Buddha's death includes a figure who looks
distinctly un-Tibetan, in fact rather more like a Sikh truck driver. 'Yes',
said Pema when I asked him about it, 'I included him because the Buddha
lived and died in India, not Tibet, and there are Sikhs in India. We are all
part of a larger religious community.' It hardly seemed to matter to him
that Sikhism had not been founded at the time of the living Buddha. Of
greater relevance was perhaps the fact that an Indian Army camp lies at the
perimeter of the monastery compound and since one-tenth of the Indian

◀ Pema Namdol Thaye, detail of a Sikh, *The Buddha's Death*

▶ Goncar Gyatso *Red Buddha*

Armed forces are Sikhs it would be prescient to keep on the right side of them. In fact an image of Guru Nanak sits amongst the portraits of Tibetan lamas on the altar at Zangdrak Palri – a gift from a visitor and a symbol of Buddhism's ecumenical spirit. Since Pema and his colleagues are no longer surrounded by Tibetans and Mongols in their daily lives it makes perfect sense to them to include the different characters and physiognomies of what has become their new environment.

If and when the exiles return home they must also consider artistic developments within Tibet itself. Over the last ten years there have been attempts, under Chinese auspices, to reconstruct and repaint some of the major monuments of Tibetan Buddhism, such as the monastery of Samye and the Jokhang in Lhasa – though the motivation for this work may well have more to do with tourism and foreign currency than with a genuine desire to right some wrongs and rejuvenate the indigenous culture. Though some artists working on these projects have somehow retained a knowledge of traditional techniques, the younger generation of artistically minded men and women have been trained within Chinese run institutions. Their vision of new Tibetan art is likely to be at odds with artists trained in Dharamasala. The recently exiled painter Gonkar Gyatso is a case in point. Trained at art schools in Beijing and Lhasa, he later became a member of a Tibetan artists' co-operative known as the 'Sweet Tea House Group'. When the authorities insisted that some Chinese members should be taken on, the Sweet Tea drinkers disbanded and Gonkar dispatched

himself to India. Those paintings which he managed to smuggle out of the country show influences from his art-school training ranging from Analytic Cubism and Surrealism to Abstraction reminiscent of the American Colorfield painters. The use of Western art terminology is not inappropriate here since Gyatso consciously aped European movements and immersed himself in any literature he could find in China on Western

Modernism. After forays into these styles he developed his own techniques and manner but returned to Tibetan themes. However, his *Red Buddha* is only residually linked to the Tibetan tradition, since the seated form of the Buddha here is more akin to an Indian sculpted (say Guptan) model than Tibetan iconometric examples. Tibetan aesthetic criteria would be hard pushed to deal with the washes of dark colour and lack of features or any kind of detail in this work. Other pieces by Gyatso where the Buddha image has been decapitated or ripped and distorted would undoubtedly be considered scandalous and sacrilegious. But perhaps there will one day be room for a Tibetan *avant garde*. In the meantime Gonkar's work is being eagerly snapped up by Japanese dealers.

Commentators who expect a culture to become moribund once disconnected from its so-called 'roots' will be surprised by the achievements of the exiled Tibetan community. It seems that, however rapid and painful the geographical and political dislocation was, the exposure to new conditions has led to everything from a subtle reinvention to a brutal restructuring of Tibetan cultural identity. Though contemporary Tibetan art has been included in shows like *Magiciens de la Terre* it does not easily fit into a postmodernist agenda but its exponents are internationalists *par excellence* though they became such *per force*. After all, the only 'state' a refugee can live in is Flux – and who knows where that is?

Shame

From The Trilogy

Jamelie Hassan

Jamelie Hassan was educated at the University of Mustansyria, Baghdad, University of Windsor, Canada, École des Beaux-Arts, Beirut, and the Academy of Fine Arts, Rome. She has exhibited widely including the OR Gallery, Vancouver (1992), Jordan National Gallery of Art, Amman (1992) and the Grey Art Gallery, New York (1991).

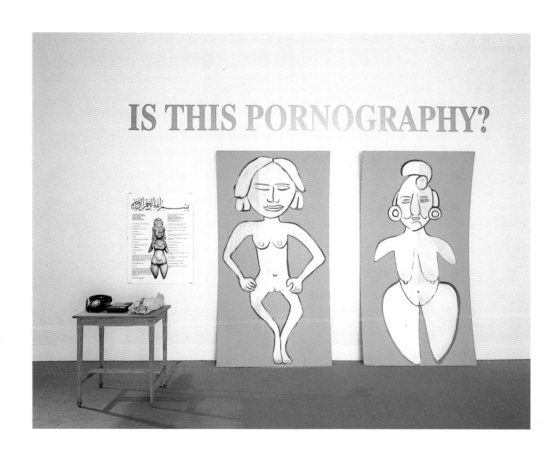

بسم الله الرحمن الرحيم

**Excerpt from transcript of
US customs inspection
Jamelie Hassan
Brownsville, Texas
Saturday, 25 July 1987**

Q. I noticed your name is Arab.

A. That's right.

Q. Where were you born?

A. Canada.

Q. You from Arabia?

A. No.

Q. What country are you from?

A. Canada.

Q. Where your parents from?

A. Lebanon.

Q. Is this your bag?

A. Yes.

*Asks me to step closer while he goes
through my handbag still holding my
passport. After checking through the
pockets of my wallet he throws everything
down on the customs table, proceeds to the
suitcase.*

Q. Who's bag is this?

A. Mine.

*Pulls out a white dress then a bag
containing two brown wrapped parcels.
He appears to look satisfied. Opens the
package. Looks disgusted. Examines the
three figures. Sets them down. Asks a
second customs man to look at them.*

Q. Is this pornography?

**Excerpt from Persian romance
Layla and Majnun
Nizami, Hakim Jamal al-din
Abu Mohammed Ilyas ibn Yusaf
ibn Zaki Mu'ayyad
Ganjey, 584 AH /1188 AD**

Woman does not keep her
promise – not even one in a
thousand.

Woman does only what satisfies
her.

Woman is faithless from the
beginning to end.

Woman loves you – until the next
man appears on the horizon.

Woman is more lustful and
passionate than man.

Woman is not trustworthy.

Woman is a cheat.

Woman is deceitful.

Woman is perverse.

Woman causes suffering; fidelity is
not her game.

Woman is peace on the surface;
she is turmoil within.

Woman's enmity is destructive.

Woman's friendship corrupts.

Woman's qualities are too
numerous to count.

David Hirsh

Darrel Ellis

On the Border
of Family and Tribe

Darrel Ellis was born in the Bronx in 1958 and got his art training at the Cooper Union School of Visual Arts, New York. His awards include the National Studio Program, The Institute for Art and Urban Resources, PS1, 1979-81, The Whitney Independent Study Program, 1981-82 and the New York Foundation for the Arts Fellowship, 1991. His work was seen in *New Photography 8*, Museum of Modern Art, New York 1992 and in a variety of exhibitions going back to 1981.

Since 1988, David Hirsh has chronicled the emergence of Lesbian and Gay representation in all its diversity in primarily American art. His hundreds of published articles are almost always based on interviews with the artists. He also videotapes interviews with artists who are lesbian or gay for public access Manhattan television. He is weekly art reviewer for *New York Native* and New York correspondent for *Euros* (Berlin).

A critical debate about families now saturates New York, with some fierce jolts. New York's Governor Cuomo probably would be US President now, had he wished, largely due to his 1980s oratory concerning 'The Family of New York'. As awareness grew that 'traditional', heterosexual two-parent families encompass only seventeen per cent of New York City's people, a knock-em-dead political battle about how the idea of family is taught in public schools (to its mostly black and Hispanic students) has become spotlit. There's also been a publicised scrutiny of specifically black families in the city, which places them collectively near 'total collapse'. Young black males on New York streets have a higher mortality rate than they had on the Vietnam battlefield.

Darrel Ellis painted, drew and photographed mostly his own extended family. He is 'best known' for his manipulations of his natural father's family photographs. His father had been killed by two policemen under odd circumstances shortly before Ellis himself was to have been inducted into the police force. Darrel, born in the South Bronx section of New York City, died at age 33 in 1992 from complications of AIDS. His undressed body laid in bed for days before being found. He had developed, after intense struggle, a primary self-love which becomes the most prized

The work of Darrel Ellis was made available to this project by Allen Frame, New York, who is looking after the estate

▲ *Artist's mother, father and sister*, 32.4 x 33.0 cm, ink and gouache on paper

◄ *Artist's mother, father and sister*, 27.9 x 35.6 cm, silver gelatin print

▲ *Artist's mother, father and sister*, 22.9 x 31.1 cm, ink and charcoal on canvas

possession of many people with terminal illnesses.

It might be said that Ellis went through three phases of 'family' during his life. First there were the blood relatives. As a child with limited materials, he absorbed himself in dreams and drawing ('especially all sorts of tiny cars', the ultimate youth symbol of getting away, moving on), eventually coming to concentrate on the human figure, primarily his relatives.

Next there was his gay family which, for him, became defined in terms of late-night clubs, day-time shopping trips and dressing in fine clothes. He later saw this as emerging from 'my need to separate myself from my family'. He served as a model for Robert Mapplethorpe, Peter Hujar and others interested in visually defining approaches to gay life, among other things. Much if not most of Darrel's own work from this period he destroyed.

If this work still existed, it would no doubt be an eloquent examination of that nebulous area which many lesbian and gay people (and many other minorities) explore in depth, the border areas between family and community or tribe. As it is, the destroyed work is one more 'hole' in

▲ *Artist's mother*,
21.0 x 27.9 cm,
silver gelatin print

◀ *Artist's mother, sister
and father*, 22.9 x 25.4 cm,
ink wash on paper

▲ *Artist's mother*, 27.9 x 35.6 cm, silver gelatin print

◀ *Artist's mother*, 62.2 x 64.1 cm, acrylic, ink, gouache and charcoal on canvas

▶ *Artist's sister*, 45.7 x 60.3 cm, ink wash, charcoal

▶ *Artist's mother*, 71.1 x 58.4 cm, ink, wash and pencil

▶ *Artist's sister,*
27.9 x 35.6 cm,
silver gelatin print
with watercolour

Ellis's art. And even as the work does exist, all of the above issues are at the heart of Ellis's art and life, joined under a solid belief in the possibility of creating Beauty which can effect both a public and private enlightenment.

After he had developed AIDS, Darrel embraced a spiritual family. As he said:

I chose for myself to distance myself from a gay identity. The particular path of spirituality which I chose to follow has made me separate myself from sexuality, period. He discovered a fine, rare balance between idealistic energy and reality, between celebration and loss. Looking backward at both art history and his own life, he filled the voids he found with an ambiguous and multi-layered luminosity.

Following are joined excerpts from the only interview which Darrel Ellis gave during his life:

I keep saying, one day I'm going to read some poetry and really get into it, so I could make better pictures. I want the work I make to effect people, which means a certain amount of rawness, getting under your skin. It's getting harder and harder to effect people anymore with images, with pictures. So many things which should have effected us was were nullified or numbed or disempowered during the crazy 1980s economics, the raw materials of those times. Who knows – but I would like to effect people as an artist.
My work is real. This is me, Darrel Ellis, and this is my family, and we're alive, emotionally very alive. I want that raw feeling, in a way very primitive and egotistical. This is one thing that connects us as human beings, this vulnerability

▲ *Party scene*,
27.9 x 35.6 cm,
silver gelatin print with
watercolour and ink

in life. I want to delete the separation between how I create, how I feel, and the viewer. We're all one human being, really.

For all my higher aspirations, I'm still a part of this society. It's no coincidence that I've chosen my family as a subject. It does relate to the broader issues of the day. A black artist who works with black images is rare. That's what effects me. I can't help but see [social] parallels when I look at those distorted pictures of black family life. In a way, of course, all families have the disruption of this lack of unity – holes, as it were. But the black family is such a big issue today, and in a way there is no black family anymore. And that's part of my reverie – I grew up with that. When I look at those photographs sometimes, all I see is holes. Sometimes I can't take it, I guess because it reflects a reality. There's a search for a wholeness, a completeness, which doesn't exist.

▶ *Artist's father,*
33.0 x 26.0 cm,
ink wash on paper

The photos show picnic scenes, family gatherings on beautiful days, black women being happy. Everything is upbeat. There's a strong juxtaposition of an ideal black, family life with all these disjunctions and holes. My father's photographic work was the raw material I needed to talk about the reality of this being gone, that it doesn't exist anymore.

I still feel that there's so much racism in the art world. People don't know how to react to you or your work, as a black artist, a lot of times. I also appreciate the fact that my voice is a lone voice and that's a very personal voice. It's like Edouard Vuillard, who I adore, in the 1990s. Bonnard and Munch and those paintings of their families – I mean, I just always assumed that that's where art came from anyhow. I didn't know any better. The race thing is a big issue and it's one I guess I really don't think about often, even though I know that it's there. Maybe I should look at it more.

I grew up loving the European tradition of art, it's my true love. In a way, it's a contradiction, being a black artist with very European sensibilities. Somehow, the photos of my family, they're very subversive in a way – subversive to me. They're challenging my whole belief system and realities.

And it's probably true, being gay will probably be my sensibility until I die. When I say gay – it's a unique perception. I felt that as a teenager and it's still the case.

I'm a free spirit.

Sutapa Biswas

White Noise

Sutapa Biswas was born in India and studied Fine Art at the University of Leeds and the Slade School of Art, London. Her work has been seen in a range of solo and group exhibitions since 1985 at the Institute of Contemporary Art, the Photographers' Gallery, Camden Arts Centre (London), OR Gallery, the Banff Centre for the Arts, OBORO (Canada), the Centre for Photographic Studies and Camerawork (USA). She lives in London.

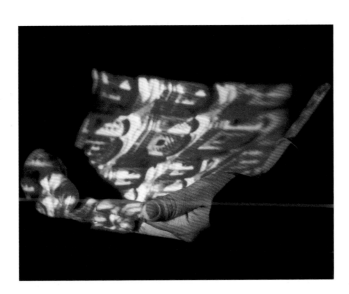

stream ~v.t.i.~ a running water; a river or brook or rivulet

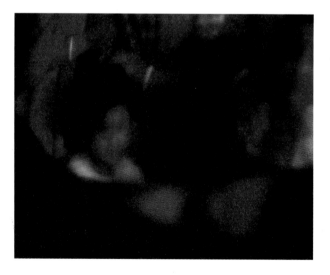

murmur -n. - an indistinct sound; a rustling from
the heart

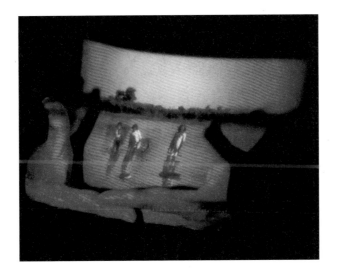

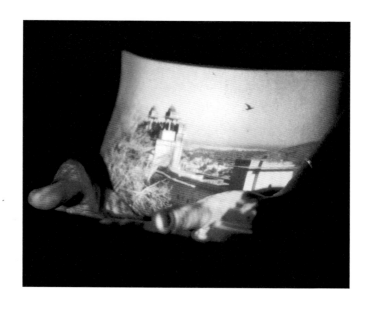

disclose ~v.i.~ to bring to view to touch stone like the menace
of angels half here half there sings

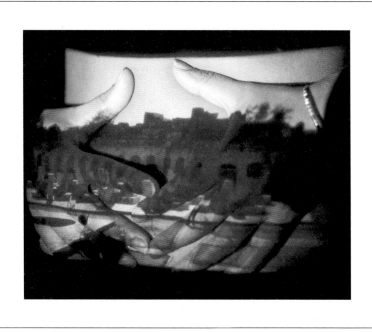

Race and Gender?

Timon Screech

Timon Screech took a BA in Oriental Studies (Japanese) at St John's College, Oxford and a PhD in Art History at Harvard. He teaches the History of Japanese Art at the School of Oriental and African Studies (SOAS), University of London.

Human Categorisation in Japan

The early-modern system

The Japanese word for a person is *hito*. This is often rendered into English as 'man' – incorrectly. *Hito* means an unspecified person.[1] Japanese lacks personal pronouns and gender-specific suffixes (such as -er and -ess) and the Japanese world as a linguistic construction is ungendered.

As with *hito*, so with the plural, *hitotachi*. The conglomeration of humanity that makes up society is flexible in terms of gender, and free of male/female binarism. Division is made of course, but by reference to other factors. In terms of the early-modern or Edo Period (1603-1868) that will concern us here, it was by what I shall refer to as 'function'. Function, similar to the Western notion of class, is hierarchical but is distinct in specifying occupation. In the West, only the bottom social rung is defined by work (it is the 'working class'). In the Japanese system all are graded in this way. During the Edo Period four 'functions' were said to exist, established by law and laid down by the shoguns in the early seventeenth-century: samurai (properly *bushi*), farmer, artisan and merchant (*shi-nô-kô-shô*). There was no word for 'function' as such, only this list. This was humanity, or at any rate, the Japanese part of it. Any other categorisation was not pertinent. All members of a family group worked together at their allotted function.

'Function' extended throughout society. There was no room for an elite exempt from the need to definite itself by activity. Unlike in China or the West, there was no notion of a 'leisured class'. To have no occupation would be to fall foul of categorisation altogether – to be an 'unperson' (*hinin*).

In some contexts, *hito* can mean 'woman'

At the top of each functional layer a cream emerged able to avoid the work proper to it, but this was no more the case with the top group than the bottom. Indeed, the bottom 'function' (the merchants) were able to built up the most conspicuous surpluses. Unlike a Western bourgeois elite, hovering in the wings waiting to move up into the next bracket, the early-modern merchants remained always merchants. However rich they became, they could not move up to the artisans (nor could an affluent artisan to move up into the farmers, etc.). There were no Dick Whittingtons. The material benefit of 'moving up' was in any case questionable, farmers being highly taxed, and *bushi* on fixed stipends eaten away by inflation.

No one acquainted with Edo society would argue that people were indifferent to gender. Gender remained a major factor in expectations and perceptions of life. But it was never the ultimate categorisation. If in the West gender is the *primary* and *least mutable* social division, in Japan that role was played by 'function'. In the West it is easier to switch class than gender; one can be classless, but to be genderless is impossible. In Japan the reverse was true.

The notion of gender   A *hito* could, if necessary, go through life undefined in terms of gender. Space was found among the intervals between male and female for such people. Those who dwelt there were not considered gender hoppers or 'halfs', though, but members of *additional* genders, neither one nor the other, but not both either. In Europe, such interstitial groups are constructed precisely as *cross*-gendered or confused. This has lead to 'homosexuals', 'hermaphrodites', 'transvestites' being subjected to quite unique degrees of opprobrium. Western society has not found room for additional genders; in Japan it did. There were several: one belonged to a most respected social group, the clergy. Buddhist monks and nuns were accounted neither men nor women, but simply 'clerics' (*sô*). To say, 'men, women and clergy' (*danjôsô*) was not to be pleonastic. Clergy lost normal gender, but were a third and they did retain normal 'function' however. Biographies of monks always specify where they hailed from among the four functions. The Western priest, by contrast, leaves rank behind, but retains gender.

To reconstruct the human categorisations of the Edo period we may refer to encyclopaedias. The most famous was the *Illustrated Sino-Japanese Compendium of the Three Geniuses (Wakan sansai zue)*, a mas-

sive work in 105 fascicle's adapted from a Chinese original and issued with diacritical markings for the Japanese reader in 1716. Seven parts address human categories. Part seven treats 'types of humanity' (*jinrin rui*, akin to function only more specific); eight lists 'family relationships' (*oya*), nine to twelve is bodily parts and medical terminology; thirteen and fourteen are foreign ethnic groups (*ikoku jinrui* and *gaii jinbutsu*). The principal divisions offered are 'type' (function), kinship (domestic hierarchy) and race. Gender is nowhere specifically treated; it occurs only in the kinship section, and even there only implicitly.

Let us consider an entry from that part:

Man, in Chinese, pronounced dan, or nan
Man: in Japanese, pronounced otoko, or vulgarly, otsuko
Husband: in Japanese pronounced masurao

The encyclopaedia gives comparative linguistics (it was based on a Chinese original) but omits gender. 'Man' is not specified as a sexual entity, and his link to 'husband' stresses a social as distinct from a gender role; 'father' (the only gender-specific aspect of the male in the family) is not mentioned. To a Western way of thinking, this definition quite misses the point.

Other entries equally render gender insignificant. 'Woman' (*menoko*) comes next, defined as, 'woman', 'wife', 'daughter', and 'old woman' (i.e. widow). The procreative aspect specific to the female sex ('mother') is absent. As with 'man', moreover, 'woman' forms one of her own sub-categories. Why? Presumably the compilers can conceive a 'woman' of the larger definition who is not a 'woman' of the lesser. If the category 'woman' means all females, the sub-category 'woman' must mean she who is neither 'wife', 'daughter' nor 'old woman', that is, a woman not located in a family. Womanhood is in part, then, to be superseded and suppressed by family position. So too is manhood.

Gender is mentioned then, only to be undermined. Insofar as it is not mentioned at all anywhere else in the *Compendium*, the reader is left to infer that gender is at best a means of structuring the home.

But gender (*sei*) does reappear in one other context in the *Compendium*, in section ten under 'uses of persons' (*jinrin no yô*). Presumably the 'use' being referred to is procreation. This section lists temporary or anomalous aspects of the *hito*, excretions, as it were, on the basic human being. Robbers (*nusubito*), lunatics (*katawamono*), disabled persons (*chinba*) and pederasts (*nanshoku*) are here too.[2]

2 This translation does not entirely cover the Japanese nuances; see below

The notion of race   Race became a matter of increasing importance from the
end of the sixteenth century after the appearance in Japan of
peoples from outside the Chinese cultural sphere. Essentially, this meant
the European powers. Japan has always considered itself ethnically pure,
and in this it draws a distinction with China and Korea, held to be racially
diverse.

The *Compendium*, having said little on gender, has a lot to
say on race. It lists enormous numbers of foreign groups. The two full sections on foreigners constitute a far larger proportion of the book than an
equivalent modern work would consider necessary. But the location of the
sections is relevant: they are placed *after* the entries on humanity proper.
That is, the reader is encouraged to doubt whether what has been said

about humanity at large pertains to
foreigners. Foreigners are not so
much parts of the larger group called
'humanity', as hived off as different
things altogether. The range (from
flying peoples to those with holes in
their chests) militated against the
reader considering them as one with
Japanese (or Chinese). The primary
point that the *Compendium* makes,
among all the welter of detail, is that
foreign types are not Sino-Japanese.
Beyond that, they are in essence a
single unit. A binary opposition
emerges in race as an 'us' *versus*
'them'. This duopoly is in distinction to the fundamental Western
duopoly, gender.

Let us consider one foreign type.
The *Compendium* mentions 'Red

▲ A folding screen,
showing the world

▲ A folding screen,
showing Japan

Primitives' (*kôî*), said to live to the north-east of Vietnam. In the few lines
at their disposal, the encyclopaedists strive to give the salient features of
this group, purging all otiose data. Gender is accordingly cropped from the
debate. Male and female among the Red Primitives are assumed to be the
same.

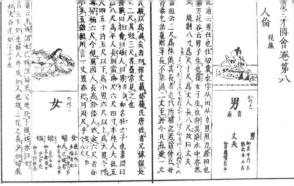

The *Compendium* is illustrated, and the pictures might have made up for this treatment by depicting a Red Primitive male and female. But they do not; only a male is given. Probably space was a relevant concern (the book is already enormously long), but more significantly, I think, gender, not seeming important, has not been registered. What is important is that these are not Sino-Japanese, they are 'primitives'.

▲ Red Primitives' (*kôi*) from *Illustrated Sino-Japanese Compendium of the Three Geniuses* (*Wakan sansai zue*)

In the illustration the Red Primitive is seen wearing his typical dress – silken skirt and crown-like cap. But what does the female wear? No clue is given. But at the time the *Compendium* was being printed these questions were indeed being raised. I shall argue that it was precisely the need to know more about foreign ethnic groups that brought gender to the fore, though introducing gender binarism jarred with the historic racial binarism.

Let us compare the illustration of the Red Primitive with another image. Here we see a radically different state of affairs. Although produced before the *Compendium* in the early seventeenth century, this work illustrates a later way of thinking. It is predicated on genders: both have now been supplied. We see, for example, a pair of Thais (*Shamu-jin*, equated in the text with Cambodians), man and woman, differing in dress and aspect, standing to demonstrate together the category 'Thai'. This couple comes from a series of doubled figures arranged like a frame around a world map. The map itself is one of a pair of folding screens, the other showing Japan, but with more foreigners in the margins. The screen suggests to the viewer that to understand the races of the world, we must know the differences between male and female.

▲ A pair of Thais (*Shamu-jin*). From *Illustrated Sino-Japanese Compendium of the Three Geniuses*

The revolutionary nature of this map, both in the treatment of the figures and in the cartographical projection is to be accounted for by the fact that it was copied from an imported original. What is being presented here is a European interpretation of the world: a European concept of race plotted on a European projection of the world. The practice of adding representative human exotica to maps was standard practice in Europe (this was, after all, the age of European expansion, and consumers at home wanted images of 'discovered' peoples) but if to Western audiences it went without saying that both sexes had to be depicted, it was startling to a Japanese viewer to see male and female written across the surface of the globe in this way.

The Japanese viewer would have been particularly arrested at the bottom of the fifth panel from the left showing Japan, for there the Japanese race is shown. Both man and woman are seen. The idea that 'the Japanese' were to be understood by reference to a male and female is a Western representation of Japaneseness, and being novel, it would no doubt have carried little conviction. The two-gender model was never altogether accepted in Japan. Neither, ultimately, was the de-binarisation of race. And yet, this map (and others like it) shows that the flipping of gender and race in human categorisation did enter the country as a potential.

Extra genders or extra races?

Extra genders

Across the world, the two-gender model is found generally plausible today. Certainly modern medicine teaches it. Accordingly, we allow a diversity to race. But in the context of the time, what was at stake in the loss of extra genders or in the gaining of extra races?

During the period of open trade with the West (from the 1570s to the 1630s) many mixed-race children were born, breaching the us/them division. There are ample records of children by Western sailors and traders and Japanese women appearing in port areas, especially Nagasaki and Hirado where the offices were. The lives of these children have never been looked at in detail. They are, for the most part, sad and often short. Initially they were not much remarked upon, but in 1636, it was determined that the blood of foreigners must not be allowed to flow in Japanese veins, and the brief period of experimentation with a plural racial system in which a person could be both an 'us' and a 'them' came to an abrupt end. All mixed-race children were expelled (together with all foreign peoples except the honorary 'us' Chinese), and racial binarism was restored. The government was doing no more than a Western government would do if (as happened) it tried to remove hermaphroditism. Both binary systems attempt to forge distinctions which cultures then take as fundamentally opposing poles that ought not to be confused or mingled.

The Portuguese were expelled from Japan in 1636. It is recorded that 287 mixed-blood children (no doubt far from he full complement) were identified and dispatched forever to the Portuguese East Indies.[3] One writer painted a picture of the resulting tragedy and confusion:

Where the father was Japanese and only the mother primitive [banjin, i.e. Western], the child was suffered to remain, but in all cases where the father was primitive and the mother Japanese, the child was expelled. Sometimes a father was expelled and a child allowed to stay, sometimes a child was expelled while the mother remained; sometimes an older brother was expelled and a younger kept, sometimes a younger was expelled and an older kept. Husband and wife were divided, and older and younger sisters were separated. Many towns and households were in a state of grief, and even though they were all brute barbarians, there was not one among them who did not wring out a sleeve wetted with tears.

So much for the Portuguese children. Three years later in 1639, it was declared that mixed-race offspring of 'Red-pelts' (that is North European, supposedly ginger and furry) must leave. The letters of one girl, O-haru, survive. At the age of seventeen, she wrote to a relation: 'How many million people are born into this world? So why was it that I had to be the daughter of a foreign man? This must be my punishment for [the sins accumulated in] a past life.'

Records of mixed-race children appear occasionally thereafter; stories were told of them, and the mixed-race child, full of guile and too clever by half, became a figure of myth.[4] But 'children of Dutch seed' (*Oranda taneko*) ceased to be an acknowledged category.

If race was not allowed down the path of diversity, gender   Extra races
in Japan had always been plural. Many were legitimately
excused from gender binarism. Taking holy orders was referred to as 'leaving the household' (*shukke*) and not being 'husbands', 'sons' or daughters, clergy and nuns needed no gendered position, though their sexual existence (and needs) were fully accepted. Another such group were known by a variety of names but principally *wakashû* or *kagema*. There is no adequate English translation, which is of course the point, but we may describe them as gender-added boys, just as monks and nuns were gender-added men and women. *Kagema* were generally prostitutes, either catering for women or men. Male (like female) prostitution exists in any city, but the *kagema* is a special case for he was constructed not as male nor female, nor as both, but as a member of an extra gender.[5]

The *kagema* was defined as young, and as he aged he prob-

3 *Hyôryû kidan zenshû, Zoku Teikoku Bunko* series vol.22, Tokyo, 1890, pp.990-92. For the next two quotations, see ibid.

4 See, for example, *Kinryûzan Fukuzô jikki* (1786), by Rinshô

▲ A *kagema* on loan
to the Azabu Museum
of Arts and Crafts,
Tokyo

ably reverted to the male he had been born, but this transfer offered no problem since gender, as we have noted, was fluid. The *kagema* who never moved on was indeed the subject of precisely the same sort of joke as the Western social climber who did the reverse and jumped their class. About thirty-five seems to have been the last cut-off age, although it was usually much before that.[6]

The word *kagema* (literally 'shadow horse') derived from the *kabuki* theatre and it referred to the young hopefuls who worked off stage. The *kabuki* world was inhabited by another third-gender group, for actors were all male (women having been banned by the authorities), and cross-dressing was a necessary part of performance. Professional female impersonators (*onna-gata*) – who might well marry and whose heterosexual exploits are as famous as their homosexual ones – were however neither male nor female. Government ordinances stipulated that female impersonators must shave their forelocks (as adult men did) so that they could not pass themselves off as females. A purple head cover was used to conceal the shaven lock, and this turned into the hallmark of the female impersonator. The cloth was a symbol of third-gender status. It was adopted by many *kagema* who had no real relations with the theatre .

Unlike the clergy with their vestments and titles, the female impersonators *kagema* had little to draw on. To a degree, their image was synthesised out of a combination of male and female elements, not to form a union but to forge a new whole. Pictorial evidence (which is copious), suggests that it was the norm for *kagema* to adopt rather feminine manners (being generally too young to show – or lack – secondary sexual characteristics); but as they were employed for sexual activity, their primary sexual characteristics spoke for their maleness. The terms of endearment used in the delicately named '*kagema* teahouses' (*kagema-jaya*, i.e. brothels) reveal that inmates were not treated as surrogate females and the 'maiden names' common at this period in English gay drinking places have no parallel in Japan.[7]

The image of the gender-added boy can be seen in an illustration by Harunobu, the celebrated designer of woodblock prints, to a story by Komatsu-ya Hyakki: *The Erotic Life of Mane'emon (Kôshoku Mane'emon)*. The interior of a *kagema* teahouse is shown with a fashionable

5 This contrasts with female prostitutes who remained emphatically female

6 A 38-year-old is derided as being past it in *Nanshoku okagami*, section 7/4. For a translation of that work, see Paul Schallow, *The Great Mirror of Male Love*, Stanford, 1990, pp.267-71

7 See, Rictor Norton, *Mother Clap's Molly House*, London, 1992

man passing time with a *kagema*. Somewhere in the central gutter that cuts through the image the *kagema* shifts from female to male. In the right-hand image, the client is with a women; in the left, with a man. Harunobu shows male and female fused, not to create a halfway-state, but to forge a new, third-gender category. In the home there are husbands and wives, old men and widows, and only male and female exist; but outside there is space for an infinite variety. The white area of the central binding is an image of the haze that covered the division between male and female in Japanese thought.

It was common for *kagema* teahouses to be near either to **Dangers** theatres, as might be expected, or to temples. Monks were debarred from sexual activity with women on pain of exile, but they were permitted to consort with boys. One of the most widely read books on the theme of inter-male sexual relationships, or *nanshoku*, was Ihara Saikaku's *Great Mirror of Nanshoku*, published in 1687. It devotes nearly a third of its short love stories to relations between monks and youths (*wakashû*, *kagema* and temple novices).[8] *Nanshoku* had supposedly been invented by the famous monk Kôbô Daishi (one of the most venerated abbots in Japanese history) and was considered the normal and appropriate outlet for monks; the comic writer and illustrator Koikawa Harumachi, jocularly defined a

◀ Harunobu, *The Erotic Life of Mane'emon* (*Kôshoku Mane'emon*), 1770

8 Ibid.

time of abnormality as 'when monks rent women and the laity rent boys'.[9]

Why was the government so stern over sex with women (*joshoku*) but so permissive over *nanshoku*? The question has great bearing on our understanding of gender. Surely being neither male or female in themselves, monks could involve themselves with similarly third-gender partners without danger. If a monk slept with a woman, he acted as a male, making a mockery of his severance of family ties, but with a third-sex partner, he was free from the danger of slipping into a male (hence 'husband') state. Sexual relations between a monk and a *kagema* was to the shogunal governments what lesbianism is in English law: a non-act.

If the monk's third-genderedness came from his having 'left the family'; the female impersonator's came from his other life on the stage; where did the *kagema's* come from? I believe this is to do with sexual practice. All the evidence suggests that active and passive roles were not reversible in a *nanshoku* relationship. The *kagema* were always penetrated. This meant that they acted in a 'non-male' way during intercourse. 'Sodomy', which in English and US law marks the single most inadmissible act, in Japan too was what ejected the recipient out of the male sphere. The penetrated did what no man would do in procreative intercourse. He did what no 'husband' did, and though possessing the means of penetration, he refrained.

Penetration of a client by a *kagema* might have occurred, but it was never part of the representation. Penetration of a lay client would have had the serious effect of sending that man into a liminal area which, as potential (or perhaps actual) father, he should not occupy. By penetrating, the *kagema* might also mark his own demise as he ran the risk of being propelled out of his third sex into the realm of men.

Nanshoku was never defined as *of itself* relevant to gender, There were none of the 'mollies', 'nancies', 'mary-annes' or the pseudo-women of the European discourse on same-sex partnership.

In around the year 1700, Yamamoto Jôchô, a formulator of thinking about warriorhood and manliness, decried what he perceived as the decline of vigour among Japanese males. He rather favoured *nanshoku* though; it was one of the hallowed activities of the battlefield, and was thought rather to enhance than detract from virility (always provided the warrior was the one who penetrated).

Given this understanding of *nanshoku*, it is not surprising that Japanese sources were baffled by the blanket European condemnation

9 *Muda iki*, reproduced in *Edo no parodei ehon*, vol.1, Tokyo, 1980, p.124

10 *Kômô zatsuwa, in Bunmei genryû sôshô*, Vol.1, Tokyo, 1917, p.467

of homosexuality. Morishima Chûryô, younger brother of the Shogunal Physician and a man of very high rank (as well as a famous rake), wrote on the subject in his book on Western matters, the *Red-pelt Miscellany* (*Kômô zatsuwa*), published in 1787. Most of the book is laudatory to excess, but under the heading, 'On the Prohibition of *nanshoku* in the West', Chûryô states:

> *In their land, nanshoku is prohibited on the most stringent terms. They say people who do it are contrary to the principles of the universe (ri) and so they make it into a crime, even now. Those found guilty can be burned to death. A young boy was found guilty and drowned in the sea – these things still occur. I heard as much only this year from the scribe Ricardo.*[10]

How the scribe came to be expatiating on this subject to high-ranking samurai would be interesting to know.[11]

Conclusion

The ban that so perplexed Chûryô is linked to the importance attached to gender in the West. So vital was gender thought that no muddying, duplicating, or crossing were ever acceptable. The more fluid apportionment of gender in Japan, and the subsidiary role alloted it in human categorisation, meant that same-sex involvement entailed no breach of an important division. Some varieties of behaviour between men might affect gender and interfere with the family, but unless a man who made his body like that of a woman while hoping to retain his male gender, there was no alarm; he could leave his gender if he chose. By contrast, race in Japan was not to be tampered with. Other than the brief period of mix, crossing race was not tolerated. Robert Adams, a member of the English trading station in Hirado, remarked in 1620, 'when women have children heere [by us], if they will keepe them they may; if the will kill then, they may.'[12] Shortly afterwards they would be obliged to kill them.

Human categorisation is always complex. I have attempted to compare two possibilities, race and gender, and show how these are not the same in all cultures. Both in the East and West though, weight was placed on one of the pair at the expense of the other, and as one was held in a firm binary grip, the other was allowed to proliferate.

11 The three senior officers of the Dutch trading station (the captain, the scribe and the physician) attended Edo almost annually. Chûryô says the meeting took place 'last year', presumably 1786. There is no record of Ricardo, but the data concering the scribes (as distinct from the other two officers) is incomplete. The topic may have come up for discussion with reference to an infamous witchhunt that had occured in Amsterdam in 1730, although such events were regrettably common, and not only in The Netherlands (Ricardo may not have been Dutch). The scaffold, not the stake, was however the usual punishment

12 Quoted in Derek Massarella, *A World Elsewhere*, Princeton, 1990, p.281

Monika Baker

Monika Baker is a
filmmaker/photographer
living in London. She is a
founding member of
Autograph — the Association
of Black Photographers, and
a director of Camerawork,
London and WAVES (an
organisation involved with
the promotion of the work of
women in film and television).
She curated, amongst other
shows, *Reflections of the
Black Experience*, Brixton
Art Gallery, London and
co-curated *Autoportraits*,
Camerawork, London.
Baker's exhibitions include:
Birthright, and the film, *Silent
in the Crowd*, winner of a First
Prize in the Black Filmmakers'
Hall of Fame Awards, 1992,
Oakland, USA. She lives in
London.

Camping Out

Self expression through mode of dress has used both liberated and repressed visual codes in making statements across boundaries. Collectively it can attack deep-rooted traditional values that effectively challenge the foundation of society, and expose the bigotry of it. The female form has always been appropriated by society as a barometer for its morals. The responsibility of woman as mother, wife, daughter or even as sister to dress according to cultural codes of behaviour may vary according to society but the message is always patriarchal domination.

Women have always subverted dress codes to politicise feminist struggles, whilst reclaiming their bodies. The nineteenth century 'bloomers' worn by radical young women became the fore runner of trousers for women. It took nearly another century before the trousers suit for women was an accepted, not fetish or camp dress code.

Accepted codes of 'moral' dress for women become more insignificant and the virgin/whore, butch/femme imagery is incorporated into one form, that is worn by the same women, thus creating confusion whilst expressing a confident sexuality. Mad, bad or dangerous women no longer dress to impress the opposite sex but to define their power. They now seek through dress codes, a self expression in terms of gender hegemony.

The rise in cross-dressing by men cannot be separated from this new confidence in contemporary women, the rules no longer apply. A man in drag can now express pleasure in wearing a frock and can allow himself to be seen in daylight. The wearing of the frock in itself is not

Colour R-Type Prints,
variable sizes

particularly progressive, after all it is mainly in Western culture (excluding Scotland) that a form of skirt/robe is not worn by the male population. What is important is the adoption by men of women's clothes. Cross-dressing, although thought to be a predominantly homosexual activity is not exclusively so. The crowned queen of the Alternative Miss World 1981, Michael Hayes, was known by friends to be heterosexual.

'High camp' is both parody and pathos, it is confrontational and a way of challenging perception. Men in drag put on a mask to act out a fantasy that is not necessarily identifiable in femininist terms. Interestingly there is no equivalent cross-dressing for women. To achieve the same sense of liberation and freedom, to push against conformity, women must outcamp the high camp. 'Madonna' and her clones are a testament to this.

The sexual revolution may have had its emphasis changed due to the HIV/AIDS epidemic, now male vulnerability and openness is encouraged with female sexuality and power/independence back in question (post contraceptive-pill 1960s).

As the wider population of men struggle in their decision to show their legs, wear lip gloss or carry a handbag without diminishing their masculinity, women will continue to advance the debate on their right to dress against conformity, and not be punished for it.

Sheba Chhachhi

Wild Mothers

Khepis and Matajis

Sheba Chhachhi works with
a variety of mediums –
photography, graphics,
audio-visuals, sculpture,
painting and performance.
An active feminist, her
photo-documentation of
the women's movement in
Delhi was shown as part of
the Spectrum Women's
Photography Festival,
London, 1988. Excerpts
from an experiment in
alternative photographic
practice, *Feminist
Portraiture – 4 Women*,
were exhibited as part of
An Economy of Signs,
Photographers' Gallery,
London (1990).

An iconographic work on women ascetics which brings together historical and contemporary representations using poetry, song, narratives, photo portraits, repproductions of folk, classical and popular art, as well as painted/sculptural images created as a response to encounters with such women.

The piece seeks to re-member and vitalise our relation with a relatively unexpressed territory of female experience – a territory mined with patriarchal oppositions between sexuality and spirituality, body and soul, sacred and profane.

The portraits, which form the core of the piece are a homage to these mothers, the product of an invitation to them to collaborate in their own representation. The work focuses on women of heterodox religious traditions: Baul, Sakta, Sufi, in Eastern India. Using the visual modes of popular art prevalent in religious sub-cultures they investigate the tension between how such personages have been imaged and how they choose to represent themselves.

This work forms a series of statements and reflections on themselves by women who dare to define themselves in relation to the metaphysical rather than the social.

Called *Khepis* (ecstatic/crazy ones), *Matajis* (spiritual mothers rather than biological ones), *Yoginis* (who seek union with the divine),

Not one, not two,

not three or four,

but through

eighty-four

hundred thousand

yonis have I come,

I have come

through unlikely

worlds, guzzled on

pleasure and on

pain.

Mahadevi Akka,

12th century AD

The Wound is the Eye Jater Ma (Mother Dreadlocks)

From *Wild Mothers: Khepis and Matajis*

Not one, not two,

not three or four,

but through

eighty-four

hundred thousand

yonis have I come,

I have come

through unlikely

worlds, guzzled on

pleasure and on

pain.

Mahadevi Akka,

12th century AD

Vacana by Mahadevi Akka excerpted from *Speaking of Shiva*, trans. A.K. Ramanujan, Penguin Classics
London, 1973

I have seen her,
a woman
crazy with love
I saw her
I saw her
right here
in this world.
Intoxicated,
she stole
the stuff of love
intoxicated,
she roams
these very paths.

She met no mate
How did she learn to love?
A maiden,
how did her womb grow
full?

these are dangerous women. Women who, while functioning within a traditional culture, question and subvert the
assumptions underlying the domestication of women.

    Religious images today, including those of
female power and divinity, are increasingly appropriated
and abused by fundamentalist ideologies in their desire to
further control the lives, bodies , minds and imagination of
both women and men.

    This work seeks to offer an independent,
personal relation to female religious figures – a critique, a
celebration and an offering.

She gave birth to three;
Two housholders,
one renunciate.
Creator
Preserver
Destroyer
She, the mother of them
all.

Yes, I have seen her,
the woman crazy with love
The one
who stole the stuff of love
I saw her
roaming these very paths.[1]

1 From a Baul song
by Radhashyamdas Gosain

Surrender in Uniform

Doug Ischar was born in Honolulu, Hawaii and grew up on naval bases in Florida and California. He received an MFA in Photography at California Institute of the Arts in 1987. His large-scale, multi-media installations use still, video photography and text to explore North American mythologies and gay male desire. His work has been exhibited at Artists' Space, Blum Helman Gallery (New York), Los Angeles Contemporary Exhibitions, the List Center for the Visual Arts(MIT) and Camerawork(London). He is Assistant Professor of Photography at the University of Illinois, Chicago.

153

Surrender in Uniform was first shown as part of *Reframing the Family* (19 January – 1 March 1991) at Artists' Space, New York, NY. It explores the lives of my parents – and my life as a child – in the context of the mythology of 1950s America. The light-box groupings are a personal and idiosyncratic synthesis of that mythology as reclaimed from childhood memories. This aspect of the work emphasises my relationship to my father. The groupings of 5x7

colour photographs construct an inventory of the artefacts of our lives, with an emphasis on the multiple roles played by my mother.

The light box images consist of colour laser copies on matte mylar. Each box contains a 'sandwich' of from two to four monochrome copies which together produce the image's final colour. The light boxes are built of dry-wall studs; the images are tied into the corners of the boxes with twine. The small colour photographs (Type-C prints) are displayed behind acetate in individual frames on glass shelves.

Dollie Mae Brothertin grew up in the small town of Electra, Texas. Her twin sister Ollie died in infancy; her mother died of appendicitis when Dollie was twelve. She had a child by her high-school sweetheart. The child died at birth.

After three years of nursing school in Norman Oklahoma, including one expulsion for bad behaviour, she bought a Buick convertible with money she had saved and drove to New York City alone.

Two years later she married my father and they moved to Hawaii.

Douglas Haig Ischar grew up in Wichita Falls, Texas. He was named after Sir Douglas Haig, a Scottish, first World War General. His mother died in the influenza epidemic of 1919. His father was electrocuted when he was nine; after that he was raised by relatives.

He joined the navy at sixteen and retired at fifty-three.

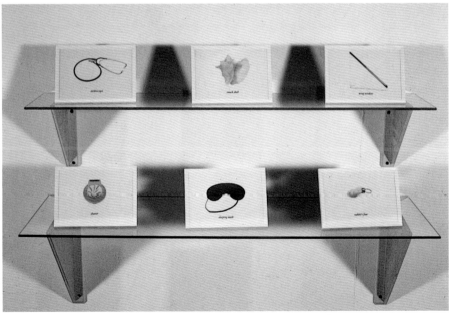

Meprobamate

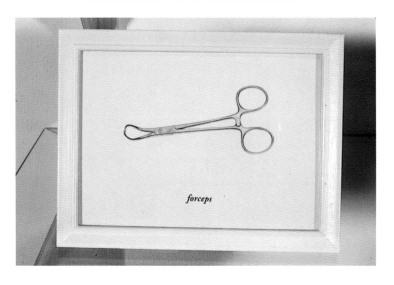

forceps

ear plugs

My mother worked as a night nurse. She would put me to bed
each night before going to work and return home as I was leaving
for school in the morning. I would wake her up when I got home
in the afternoon.

She died of cancer, a patient in the same hospital where she had
worked for twenty-five years.

My father spent six months a year at sea. I looked forward to his
returns; he sometimes brought exotic gifts.

Two years after retiring from the navy he killed himself in the
family garage. While going through his belongings my sister
found – at the bottom of his sea chest – a flowery letter of
devotion written to a man.

Disturbances

Millie Wilson

Millie Wilson was born in Hot Springs, Arkansas and lives in Los Angeles. She is Regular Faculty in the Program in Art at the California Institute of the Arts and has taught at the University of Illinois. Her work has been shown in various American galleries and museums, including: ICA, Boston, the Whitney Museum, New York, LACE, Los Angeles, the San Francisco Museum of Modern Art, Randolf Street Gallery, Chicago.

From The Museum of Lesbian Dreams

This project arises from an installation, *Fauve Semblant: Peter (A Young English Girl)*, shown at Los Angeles Contemporary Exhibitions in November/December 1989. That installation used the conceit of a museum exhibition which constructed the character of a lesbian artist in early modernism. I was able to propose her scandalous presence in history, and to invoke relevant theory, politics and practice. I was particularly interested in summoning up stereotypes in order to reposition them humorously, to invest them with power for lesbians, and to demonstrate what fictions those constructions are. So it is those stereotypes of lesbian sexuality and identity which I want to continue to explore. I don't intend to present testimonials to some notion of idealised and romantic lesbian dreaming, but I want to make use of the treatment of lesbians (in the 1950s and 1960s) in psychiatric texts written for a popular readership, such as *The Lesbian in America* by Donald Webster Cory.

In addition to a history, pseudo-scientific discourse, chapters on lesbians as prostitutes, prisoners, and patients including case studies and confessionals, such books frequently include a chapter on lesbian dreams, with emphasis on a psychoanalytic reading of dreams in the process of effecting a 'cure'. The vulgar Freudianisms are hilarious, especially when imagined in a literal way, and the work I am planning would do just that. The work would be entitled *Freud's Golden Eggs*, an would include a formal presentation of a turnip and potato, both cast in bronze, resting on a brass field engraved with the text of the dream and the citation. (One example of the interpretation of dreams involves reading a turnip as symbol of heterosexuality, and a potato as a symbol of homosexuality.) The

▲ Installation view of
*The Museum of Lesbian
Dreams: Disturbances*,
1990, 12' x 20', silver
gelatin prints and
silkscreens

ensemble would be covered with a plexiglass box and exhibited on a pedestal. Another piece would be a deification of penis envy, and a third involves a fur-lined trophy.

With these literal transcriptions of dream symbols, I want to extend the notion to include various constructions of lesbian desire, in order to counter those descriptions from medical discourses. One work will involve photographers' glamour shots of women who were in military service in the Second World War, a tableau which includes references to the purging of lesbians in the military and the State department in the 1950s, but which also maintains an erotic charge in viewing the photos. Another piece will take a list of pathological disturbances (like facial expression and involuntary movement) which are categorised as signs, gestures and objects, and reclaim them by constructing a seductive and humorous lesbian subject.

Sadie S.

General Impression:

The attitudes and behavior of Sadie suggest an energetic young boy. She is a twenty-nine year old woman of medium height and weight. She has a well-shaped head and a high forehead from which her short hair is brushed briskly back. Her haircut is mannish and her clothes tailored. Her eyes are gray and languid. Her handclasp is quick and strong and her gait is firm, almost a strut.

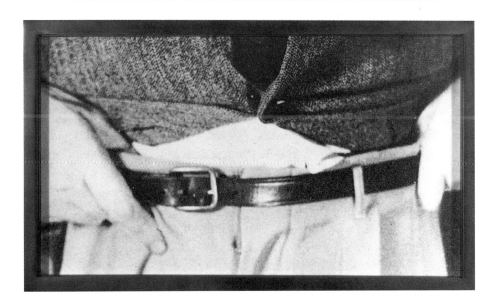

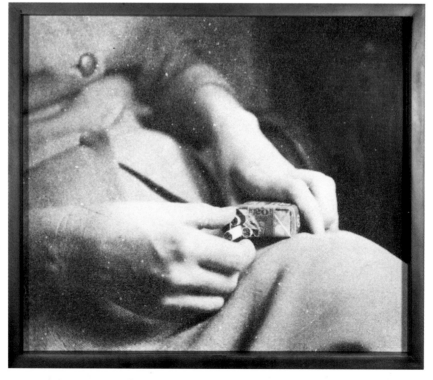

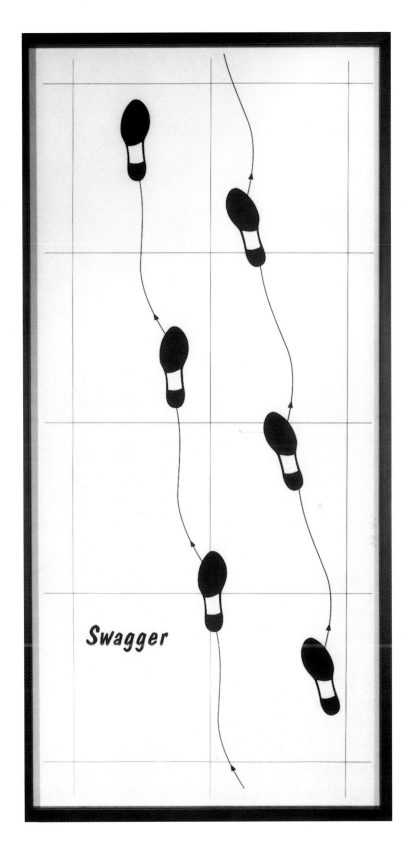

Swagger

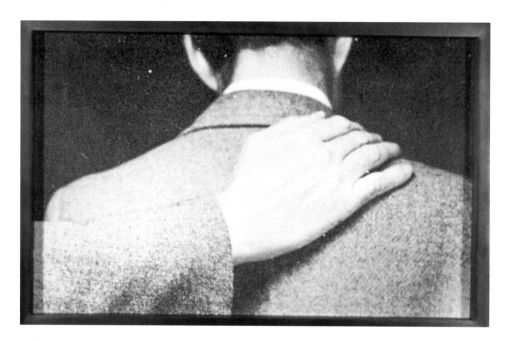

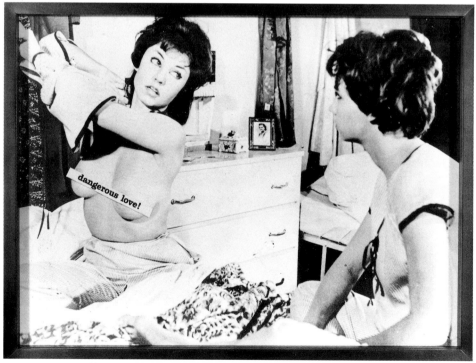

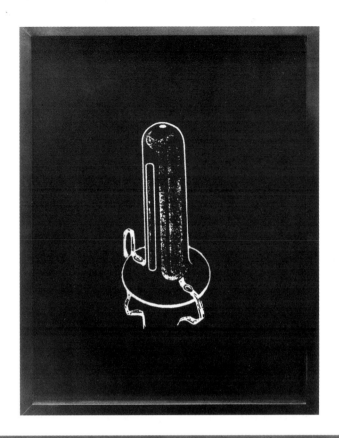

The Flow of Water

Samena Rana

Photographer, teacher, translator and traveller, Samena Rana touched many lives with her energetic presence. She came to England from Pakistan for medical treatment and after completing A levels, she worked in Saudi Arabia as a translator. On her return to London, she enrolled on a photography course after which she started a campaign for wheelchair access to a darkroom at Camerawork in East London. While teaching English as a second language and disability awareness, Rana exhibited work in several shows, including *Darshan*, a black artists' exhibition at Camerawork, and *Crossing Black Waters*, at the South London Art Gallery.

On identity

As far as my own identity is concerned, I see myself as a Pakistani who's been living in Britain for 20 years. I'm a product of the two cultures and I don't know where one begins and the other ends. I think in the colours that surround me – a lot of my (South) Asian identity comes through – and hence, my photographs are of Lahore because that's where my inspiration lies.

Lahore means a lot to me. Although I've been in England for 20 years, Lahore is a place where I feel comfortable. In Pakistan, people really care about each other – their warmth makes me forget about the wheelchair. People are helpful without making a big deal about it, even though it's not very accessible over there. Visually, I adore the colours – what people wear, the shops, the street, the bazaar.... Everything is simple there, with a lot of imagination. Because I live in England, where everything is very, very different, I appreciate the culture far more than if I had stayed there.

I am Pakistani. That is vital to my being and reflects all around me. But there is a Western influence when I choose friends, etc., but I'm still exploring where I'm at – where my loyalties lie if I have any loyalties. I'm quite confused by the process. I hate them (labels). When I first exhibited as a 'black' photographer, I had never thought of myself as black. I didn't know any Asian people until four years ago. I thought Asian people would not be able to relate to me, since I was Westernised and disabled. But there are some things my white friends could never relate to either. Twenty

The estate of Samena Rana is represented by *Panchayat*, London, who facilitated this contribution

years went by without my learning anything about Pakistan, but I'm now learning Urdu, reading poetry, and listening to music. A lot still needs sorting out.

I never used to see myself as a disabled person because in **On (dis)ability** my dreams I used to walk. I don't view myself as a full-time disabled person. From the beginning, I've always been on the edge of things. I'm never in the middle – I can't be pigeon-holed.

I do want to see the disability movement go forward. But each individual has to make up their own mind as to where they're coming from. I have to do what I'm doing and if we differ, we must differ. In the disability movement, there is dialogue with different opinions and different directions. Some people want a totally segregated, disabled art, but this is too limiting for me. We need an ongoing, new movement. People are just sorting out where they are, and articulating their ideas. It's slow.

The other aspect of my photography is connected to my own disability. I'm interested in producing images of people – people and how they connect to their own environment. Often I'm quite distressed by the images of disabled people I see in the media – especially those horrible, grey posters one sees everywhere because charities want to raise money. They want to produce people's images as being grey and passive. I find this hurtful, and it makes me very angry. So I'd like to take photographs which depict disabled people as active and positive people, because that's who we are. People who are doing things – everyday things, ordinary things – but actually doing things, and not being passive.

▲ *Self Portrait*, 1992
Colour C-Type

The media can also help break down the stereotypes by finding out more about the individuals and portraying a just picture.

The main problem I can't solve is access. But I think access **On access** and the problems of access are there because of attitudes and people's prejudices – because if they really stop and think, then there is the money, there is the funding. To try and battle against people's attitudes is the hardest thing that I've found. It's an ongoing thing for any disabled person. In the field of photography it's even harder, because it is such an able-bodied, male-dominated profession.

The problem of physical access comes into everything. That is the main problem with colleges and darkrooms, and their equipment, is that they are all inaccessible.

The Arts Council and Greater London Arts ought to make a commitment in their code of practice which allows a certain criteria for financially helping disabled people. At the moment, they follow a code of practice which says how they should be helping disabled artists, but it's a token gesture – nothing practical or realistic. We don't need just token gestures, but actual commitment to disability. In practical terms, it's funding – accessible darkrooms, accessible venues, everything that is funded should include disabled people.

We need legislation against discrimination of people based on disability (like American legislation). It's a commitment needed by the government and to be passed down – not a code of practice that simply remains on paper.

On her work   I've always taken snapshots. I used to take photographs on an automatic camera with a timer because I couldn't hold the camera and press the button at the same time. At one time I would hold the camera and someone else would press the button, but this was limiting. I've struggled with obstacle after obstacle, but since 1985 I've wanted to do it on a more serious level.

I'm still searching for my influences. Through my reading, I haven't been able to find people I can relate to. But the first person I feel I can relate to is Frida Kahlo, the Mexican painter. What first attracted me to her painting was her wheelchair. She led an incredible life.

I want to compile a book of photographs about defying stereotypes of disability and of Asian women as passive, weak, meek little creatures that don't have a voice. I want to make photographs that challenge and come to some kind of conclusion.

◀ *Memories I, II, III*

▲ *The Silence IV*

◀ *Fragments of Self V, VI, VII*

▼ *Awakening VIII-XI*

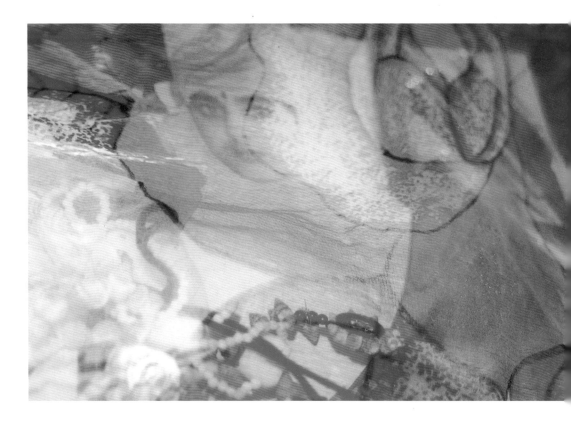

**Emily Andersen and
Renée Tobe**

The Ladies Cabinet

Emily Andersen is a graduate of the Royal College of Art, and a freelance photographer and film-maker working in London. Her work is widely published in magazines, by record companies, and in books. Her exhibitions include *The Compelling Eye* (RCA 1989), *Ecstatic Antibodies* (Impressions York, 1990, Ikon, BAC, Montreal, etc.) She is currently working on a book of women and their fathers.

Renée Tobe was born in 1960 in Toronto, Canada. She attended Ontario College of Art and Cornell University. and completed her studies at the Architectural Association in London. Renée received, with Emily Andersen, a Greater London Arts award for *The Ladies Cabinet.* She has designed a television stage set for Channel Four and created the Odyssey Tower used on an album cover by Mute Records. Renée Tobe lives and works in London.

A leather-bound volume ... the mouldering pages of an ancient tome. It opens to the smell of must and mouldy ideas. On the frontispiece is an engraving of a skeleton leaning casually against a table, a book held in one bony hand. On the title page the name of the book ... *The Ladies Cabinet – A Queen's Delight.* The book is a compilation of old remedies for a variety of needs from cures for colic to relief from pain of childbirth. This seventeenth-century publication is the inspiration for our photographs. In our contemporary world stalked by hunger, death and disease, where medical research is more likely to be funded according to the profit to be realised than the number of lives to be saved, it seems timely to cast a critical eye on the icon of medical practises both antique and contemporary.

THE
LADIES CABINET

ENLARGED and 879
OPENED:

Containing
Many Rare Secrets, and Rich Orna-
ments of several kindes, and
different uses.

Comprized
Under three general Heads.

Viz.
of
1. Preserving, Conserving, Candying, &c
2. Physick and Chirurgery.
3. Cookery and Houswifery.

Whereunto is added,
Sundry Experiments, and choice Ex-
tractions of Waters, Oyls, &c.

Collected and practised,
By
the late Right Honorable and
Learned Chymist,

The Lord RUTHUEN.

With Xou. 1st
A particular Table to each Part.

London, Printed by T.M. for M.M. G. Bedell,
and T. Collins, at the middle Temple-
Gate, Fleet-street. 1654.

Oyl of Swallows Take two dozen or twenty Swallows out of the nest, a good handful of Rosemary, as much Lavender cotton, and as much Strawberry leaves, strings and all, stamp all these together and fry them altogether in May butter, or rather sallet Oyle, til the rawnesse be gone; then put it in earthen potfast stopped nine days, and then try it again; wring it thorow a cloth, and keep it in a glass and being warmed annoint the place grieved therewith, it is good for all aches, and for the shrinking of sinews.

Oyl of Swallows

Bloody Flux Cured To ease the pain of childbirth make the representation of the whole world in a glass. Take the purist salt Nitre, as much as you please, of Tin half so much, mix them together, and calcine them hermetically; to which annex a glass receiver, and lute them well together; let leaves of gold be put into the bottom thereof, and rose petals; then put fire to the retort, until vapours arise that will cleave to the gold; augment the fire til no more fumes ascend, then take away the receiver, and close it hermetically, and make a lampe fire under it, and you will see presented in it the Sun, Moone, Stars, Fountains, Flowers, Trees, Fruits, and indeed even all things which is a glorious sight to behold.

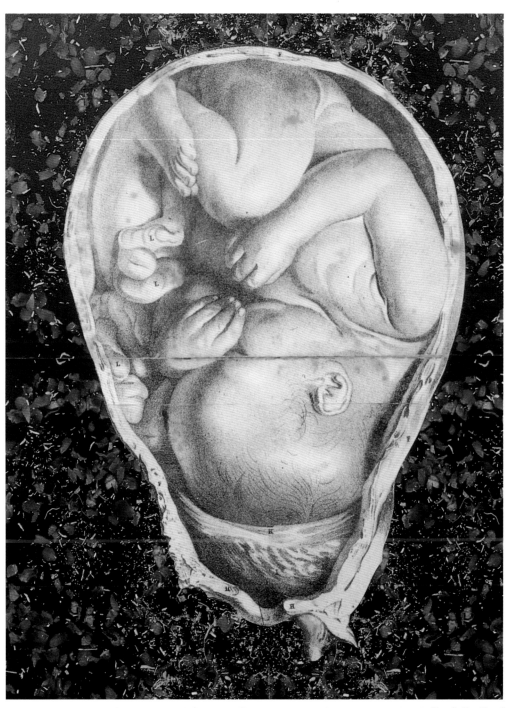

Bloody Flux Cured

To Make Water of Life   Take balm leaves and stalks, Burnett leaves and flowers, Rosemary, red Sage, Tarragon, Tormentil leaves, Bossolis, red Roses, Carnation, Hysop, Thyme, red strings that grow upon savoury, red fennel leaves and roots, red Mints, of each one hand-ful, bruise these herbs and put them in a great earthen pot, and pour on them as much white wine as will cover them, stop them close, and let them steep eight or nine days, then put to it Cinnamon, Ginger, Angelica seeds, Cloves and Nutmegs of each one ounce; a little Saphron, Sugar one pound, Raysins stoned one pound, Dates stoned and sliced half a pound, the loyns and legs of an old Coney, a fleshy running Capon, the red flesh of the sinews of a leg of mutton, four young chickens, twelve larks, the yolks of twelve eggs, a loaf of white bread cut in sops, and two or three ounces of Mithridate or Treacle, and as much Bastard or Muscadine as will cover them all: Distil all with a moderate fire, and keep the first and second waters by themselves, and when there comes no more by distilling, put more Wine into the pot upon the same stuff, and distil it again and you shall have another good water. This water must be kept in a double glass close stopped very carefully: it is good against many infirmities, as the Dropsie, Palsey, Ague, Sweatings, Spleen, Worms, Yellow and Black Jaundice; it strengthens the Spirits, Brain, Heart, Liver and Stomach. Take two or three spoonfuls when is by itself, or with Ale Beer or Wine mingled with Sugar.

To Make Water of Life

Signs of Death in the Plague   Take of Sanicle two handfuls, of Adders tongue, Doves' foot, and Sheppard's purse, of each as much, of Limuria one handful, chop them somewhat small, and boil them in Deers suet, until the herbs be crumbly, and waxe dry. If the sores be open annoint with this.

Signs of Death in the Plague

Annointment for a Rupture   Take a live frog, and lay the belly of it next to the sore; if the patient will escape the frog will burst in a quarter of an hour, then lay on another; and this you shall do til more do burst; for they draw forth the venome. If none of the frogs do burst, the party will not escape. Some say a dried toad will do it better.

Annointment for a Rupture

Objects of Sympathetic Magic   Cloth heart stuck with pins, hair and nail parings found in Greybeard jug ten to eleven feet below street level in bed of old mill stream course, under corner of Tufton Street and Great College Street, Westminster in damp soil, 1904. The cork has shrunk from drying. Sheep's heart stuck with nails and pins. Model made by an old woman who in youth prepared hearts thus to break evil spells. Object said to be a toad, stuck with thorns for witchcraft purposes; found with the heart here exhibited. Clay stuck with pins. Fish which undergoes changes under influence of warmth and moisture of the hand. Used by a father to detect culprits among his children through its behaviour on the palm of the hand. They greatly dreaded its power of detecting the guilty.

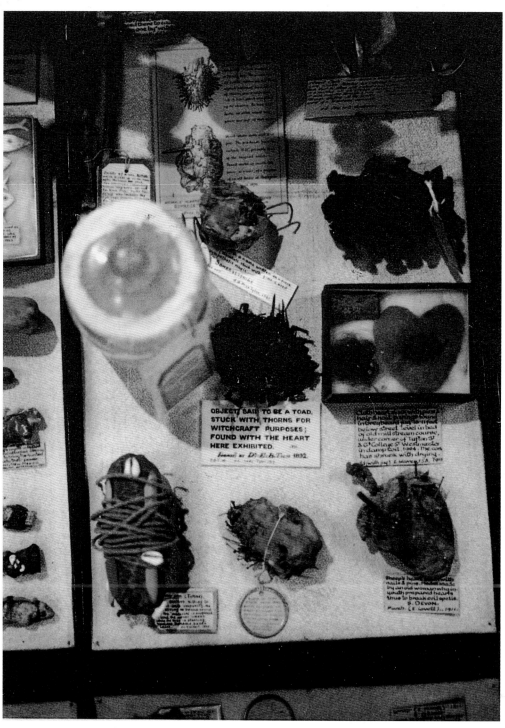

Objects of Sympathetic Magic

A Rare Secret to Cure the Same   Take the juyce of ground Ivy, Colt's foot, Stabious, Lungwort, of each one pound and a half; the juyce of Purstain, Plantaine, Ambrosia, Quince, Pauls Betony, of each a pound; Hog's blood, White wine of each four pounds, Garden snails two pounds, dryed Tobacco leaves, powder of Licorice two ounces, Alicampane half an ounce, of Onis an ounce, Cotton seeds an ounce, the greater cold seeds, Annise seeds, of each six drachms; Saffron one drachm, the flowers of red Roses six pugils, of Violets and Borage, of each four pugils; steep them three days warm, and then distil them in a glass Still in Sand.

A Rare Secret to Cure the Same

For Young Children That Are Weak in Their   Take Sage, sweet Marjoram, each a like
Limbs and Can Neither Go Nor Stand   quantity, beat them very well together and
strain out the juyce, and put it into a double vial glass, fill the glass as full as it can hold; then
stop it with paste very close, and cover it with thick paste all over, and then set it in an Oven,
and then let it stand so long as a great loaf requires time to be thoroughly baked; then take
it out, and let it be cold, then break the paste round about it, and if the juyce be grown thick,
break the glass, and put it into a gallipot and keep it. When you will use it take the quantity
of two spoonfuls at a time, and as much marrow of an Ox leg, melt them together, and
mingle them well, and both morning and evening annoint therewith (as warm as it can be
endured) the tender parts of the child's thighs and legs, and knees, chasing them well with
your warm hands; and so in a short time (through God's blessing) it will be able to stand and
go. Successfully proved.

For Young Children That Are Weak in Their Limbs and Can Neither Go Nor Stand

Sutura Velcrum   Samples of sutures and stitches to repair ruptures of the skin. As well as to reconnect skin that has been cut by the operating surgeon during exploratory surgery or when removing organs or articles embedded beneathe the surface.

Left picture. Detail the removal of a man's breast showing the fatty substance beneathe.

Right picture.Detail showing the reparation of an eye, re-attaching the lens and the rest after the removal of a foreign object embedded there-in.

 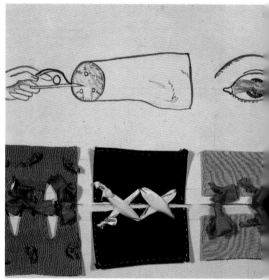

Sutura Velcrum

To Heal Children of the Lunatic Disease   This disease happeneth to children by reason of a worm with two heads, which breadeth in their bodies, which cometh to the heart, causeth such a passion in the child, that oft times it kills them. The remedie whereof is this, Dry the tender stalks of a wilding tree in the shadow; then stamp them well, and sift them, and take of the said powder, and roots of Gentian, Myrrh and long Pyome, of each a quarter of an ounce; all these well beaten to powder you must put in a dish, or some other vessel, and moisten them with a little water; then take of it with your two fingers, and wet the lips and mouth of the child: Do this three or four times, and you shall see the worm come forth dead with the excrements.

To Heal Children of the Lunatic Disease

Claudine K. Brown

An Authoritative Voice

Establishing A National African American Museum

Claudine K. Brown is Project Director for the National African American Museum Project and Deputy Assistant Secretary for the Arts and Humanities at the Smithsonian Institution. She has worked at the Brooklyn Museum, served as a Museum Educator, Manager of School and Youth Programs and as Assistant Director of Government and Community Relations. She has contributed articles to *Patterns in Practice*, *Selections from the Journal of Museum Education* and other journals.

There currently exists no single institution devoted to African Americans which collects, analyses, researches and organises exhibitions on a scale and definition comparable to the major museums devoted to other aspects of American life.
Executive Summary, September 1990

The visual image of African Americans has been a dominant concern in late twentieth-century literature, art practices and cultural institutions. The overriding issue in this discourse in 1992 focused on the establishment of a conceptually new museum which would provide an authoritative voice within the African American community and disrupt the historical notions of traditional museum history and exhibition development within this context. In establishing a voice from within the community to discuss the possibilities of re-examining and reinterpreting the diverse experiences and collected histories of African Americans; committees of scholars, artists and museum professionals gathered to explore the concept of developing a National African American Museum at the Smithsonian Institution in Washington, DC.

Over its long history, the Smithsonian has had an episodic and inconsistent track record in presenting the African American aspects of American life. In very recent years, it has tried to give a more balanced picture by presenting exhibitions on migration and the African American experience, as well as fine art exhibitions examining the life and works of African American artists active in the 1930s and 1940s. Few Smithsonian museums however have long-standing exhibitions which reflect the nation's plurality. Some have cautioned that if a door is opened by the creation of a National African American Museum, each ethnic group that makes up the American population would demand a museum. A response to that is – most descendants of European immigrants have been assimilated, physically and culturally, into white America. Racial minorities, on the other hand, have been less completely assimilated and still maintain their racial and cultural identities. To some extent, this is a reflection of bias against these minorities because of their apparent difference. However an inability to assimilate often results in a heightened appreciation of one's own cultural heritage. While we are a nation of immigrants, as Booker T. Washington said almost one-hundred years ago, Blacks are the only people who came here by special invitation. Black people have a unique history in America of toil and trouble, of achievement and institutional development that cannot easily be translated into, or subsumed under a generalised American national experience.

There is a need for a National Museum which is able to embrace a broad perspective. This includes exploring diversity within the African American experience as well as the history and culture of persons of African descent throughout the Diaspora. Diasporan studies are rarely the subject of museum research or exhibitions. We know of no curatorial department in this country that deals exclusively with this area. The same can be said of an analysis of regional difference amongst African Americans within the US. A specific goal of a National African American Museum will be to identify those areas of research which are essential to a cohesive understanding of the African American experience, but which have heretofore been neglected or inadequately funded.

This point has been made by one of America's most influential museum professional's Fath Davis Ruffins. Ruffins, a historian at the National Museum of American History at the Smithsonian maintains:

over the last thirty-five years, two generations of scholars in a variety of disciplines have detailed much about early American society and the contributions of Black people to it. In a sense, the Columbus Quincentenary marks the beginning of contact among Indians, Europeans and Africans. The African Diaspora in the Americas was a major world-changing demographic, cultural, and ecological shift. The immigration, however unwilling, of millions of African peoples was one of the single most important events shaping the world as we know it today. In the modern

From 1980 to 1992, Deborah Willis-Braithwaite was Curator of Photographs and Prints and Exhibition Co-ordinator at the Schomburg Center for Research in Black Culture. Currently Willis-Braithwaite is serving as Collections Co-ordinator for the Smithsonian Institution's National African American Museum Project in Washington, DC. Widely published, Willis-Braithwaite is the author of, among other publications, *J. P. Ball, Daguerreotypist and Studio Photographer; Black Photographers 1940-1988: An Illustrated Bio-Bibliography*; and the forthcoming publications *Picturing Us: African American Identity in Photography* and *The Portraits of James Van Der Zee*.

The Arts and Industries Building, Smithsonian Institution, about 1895

era, the arrival of Europeans and Africans in the New World is essentially
simultaneous.

Upon arrival, most Africans were enslaved. While there were a number of
Indian peoples who were enslaved and even a few Europeans, especially
before 1700, eventually slavery came to be defined as African. Although slavery ended at different times in different countries, the nearly 400 hundred
years of the institution shaped many aspects of American cultures in a variety
of ways. In the US, the Declaration of Independence and the Constitution
were deeply affected by the presence of slavery within the states. Eventually,
the only American civil war was fought, at least in part, over the question of
slavery. While many American ethnic groups have experienced prejudice and
discrimination, no groups were as formally segregated by law and in practice
as Black Americans. For the first 200 years, African-Americans have argued
for the extension of citizenship and human rights in ways that elaborated
notions of freedom for all Americans and inspired others around the world.
In the white population in the United States, more than 60 per cent are
descended from Europeans that arrived in the last 100 years, whereas more
than 95 per cent of African Americans are descended from an ancestor who
arrived prior to 1800. For all these reasons, African Americans have a unique
history within the US and within the wider Diasporic world.

      There is a need to respond to a crisis situation in the area of
collecting and preserving African American cultural patrimony. Because
museums have only recently acknowledged a need to collect African
American material, we are poised at a time in our history where important
documents and objects may be lost if we are not able to alert our communities
to the value of their personal treasures and stories. Additionally, many more
established museums are just beginning to identify and properly conserve
African American material in their collections. A National African American
Museum could co-ordinate efforts in the collecting of African American
material culture which is rapidly disappearing because of a lack of resources
and trained professionals engaged in this effort. This can be achieved in part
through the development of an African American Collections DataBase and
explore the possibility of a facility for shared collections.

      A National African American Museum in the District of
Columbus can attract tourists from throughout the country and from around
the world. The Nation's capitol is an ideal place to begin to dispel stereotypes
and change public perception about African Americans. According to a sur-
vey recently conducted by the National Opinion Research Center of the
University of Chicago, other ethnic groups perceive African Americans to be

disproportionately lazy, violent and unpatriotic.

These perceptions have historical roots and cultural antecedents which can be effectively explored in museum exhibitions and programming. The relationships which African Americans have forged, or which have been imposed upon them in this country by virtue of their involuntary migration, subsequent subjugation and continued fight for social, political and cultural equity make their story unique and therefore essential to the accurate understanding of the American experience. A National African American Museum can also draw international attention to issues of importance in the African American Museum community.

A National African American Museum at the Smithsonian can enhance and support the efforts of other Smithsonian Museums which collect, research and display African American material. The creation of a National African American Museum will not excuse other Smithsonian Museums from representing our culturally pluralistic society in their collections and interpretative programmes. Additionally, having several Smithsonian museums which interpret similar material is not unprecedented, nor is it duplicative.

The Smithsonian has a history of exploring singular issues from varied points of view. The National Museum of American Art, the Hirshhorn Museum and Sculpture Garden and the National Portrait Gallery all collect and interpret American art. Both the National Museum of African Art and the Natural History Museum collect African Art; and the Freer and the Saekler collect Asian Art. Additionally, visitors will be able to see Native American material in New York at the Customs House, at the National Museum of the American Indian on the Mall and at the National Museum of Natural History.

The scope of all of this material warrants such extensive holdings. Such is no less the case for African American art and material culture. Given the piece-meal approach to documenting the achievements of African Americans in museums throughout the country, the Smithsonian as the nation's museum is the appropriate venue for a comprehensive consideration of this material.

In an act of intervention and urgency the National African American Museum's mission would be dedicated to the collection, preservation, research and exhibition of African American historical and cultural material reflecting the breadth of experiences of people of African descent in the United States and throughout the Diaspora.

Helen Grace   Helen Grace lectures in the
School of Visual and
Performing Arts, University of
Western Sydney, Nepean,
Australia.

Pavilions of the Ego

The Critic as Art Object

There are three productive senses in which we might think about the word, 'Shift'; three senses which clarify reasons for considering the problem of art criticism. First, *Shift* might refer to a paradigm shift in a Kuhnian sense, of which we could be in the middle, a revolutionary moment in which the parameters which have operated in the last ten, twenty years or so in thinking about criticism might be shifting. In the heroic narratives of the history of ideas, the paradigm shift is a much desired state, and there are always numerous snake-oil salesmen, keen to persuade us that we are in such an historic moment and keen to provide the right set of ideas (for a price) which will help us through such a moment and into the bright future beyond it. The second sense in which we might understand the word is in terms of a kind of sideways move for the time being, a sort of evolutionary shift. Such a shift could register a declaration of irritation about a current position, a sense of wanting a change. It could represent simple shifts in consumer demand, reflecting or generating shifts in the market. In a third sense we might note that a shift is a kind of frock and we could play with this connotation in the context of debates about women priests and suggest there is a certain defrocking of priests going on; heresies have been discovered, or people have been led down the garden path by an approach that no longer holds water, and they are shouting for blood. There is something of this in the dissatisfactions in relation to art criticism a sense of growing conservatism and of absence of meaningful debate. I think of 'shift' more in terms of the second and third connotation.

In *Resisting Blackmail*, Yves-Alain Bois's introduction to *Painting as Model*, a number of pressures are identified as intellectual black-

Adapted from a paper given at the *Shift* conference, IMA, Brisbane, April 1992

1 Yves-Alain Bois, *Introduction, Resisting Blackmail in Painting as Model*, MIT Press, 1990, p.xiii

mail within humanities and art history in America. In many ways the same pressures exist in Australia, although I think there are also more interesting additional ones, Bois's comments present a more considered response than we usually see to the 'political correctness' quarrels which are taking place in the US.

Bois names the pressures, or sites of intellectual blackmail as theoreticism, anti-theory, fashion, anti-formalism, socio-political demand and asymbolia, and these terms function as a series of fairly recognisable oppositions. The first opposition Bois uses (theory/ antitheory) is concerned with the place theory occupies in universities (and to add, most emphatically, in art schools as well). It is not theory, he says, which is oppressive, but 'the indiscriminate appeal to theory as a set of ready-made tools to handle a question'. He speaks of theory functioning as a superego 'encapsulating, fuelling and ... discouraging the student's endeavour' and summarises his problem in a way which, we could appropriate as an accurate description of a situation which exists for us in art criticism:

Theoreticism, or theoretical abuse, is based on the illusion that one could ingest swiftly, without previous homework, a mass of difficult and often contradictory texts. Without the background that would permit this material to be mastered usefully, the theoreticist first gives in to 'theory' as if it were a new faith; then, more or less rapidly, grows disenchanted because 'theory' did not perform immediately the expected miracles. Illusion leads to disillusionment, disillusion to resentment, and resentment to throwing out the baby with the bath water. As a consequence of this theoretical retreat, the old guard positivists, feeling vindicated – even though they had never lost an inch of their power – re-emerge as more vociferous than ever.[1]

In the blurb for the SHIFT Conference (IMA Brisbane, 1992), theory is invoked in a manner which encompasses the kinds of dangers that Bois identifies. It is claimed that this conference 'reflects the *fact* that in many ways it is criticism and theory that have set the agenda for art in the nineties' (my emphasis) and that 'the true *avant garde* today might lie in the speculation upon art and not in art itself'. Against this, it would be easy to point out the extent to which it is indeed speculation, in a different sense, which has led to the collapse of interest in art, as the would-be collectors amongst the entrepreneurs have been forced to leave the market, leaving the more fortunate artists with large provisional tax bills and studios which are not sustainable (galleries find themselves in similar difficulties). In this context it is difficult to see how 'the speculation upon art' in the sense in which the conference flyer intends it, can itself escape the trickle-down effect of market collapse, since it is also these speculations which have served to produce some of the legitimacy attached to various practices in the market place.

Part of the reason I've used Yves-Alain Bois here has to do with the way in which he invokes Clement Greenberg, even if his own position could be seen to be opposed to Greenberg's. I'm interested in the respect accorded to Greenberg in so much of the work which ostensibly identifies him as one of the arch-villains of the last fifty years. Bois explains the context in which Greenberg came to have appeal for French art criticism, in spite of the objections which political artists in America, such as Hans Haacke could make of him:

But for us ... rather ignorant of the art-world politics in question and certainly unmoved by its local effects, Greenberg's discourse represented a serious blow to the extremely mediocre practice of French art criticism, dominated at best by the specific French phenomenon of the writer's or philosopher's essay on art, more often than not an efflorescence of condescending words uttered by a complacent man of letters.[2]

In recent years, there has been some tendency to mimic this approach, in which the writer or philosopher is called upon to be condescending before works of art but I'm less concerned about this than the continuing problem of art and its capacity or incapacity to make a difference, whatever strategies are employed to make it important, even if it doesn't make a difference.

Curiously, on one key point – the capacity of art to make a difference – opponents such as Greenberg and Haacke are in agreement. Haacke has said:

Nothing, absolutely nothing, is changed by whatever type of painting or sculpture or happening you produce .... We must face the fact that art is unsuited as a political tool.[3]

And Greenberg has been similarly emphatic:

It simply is a fact that I don't see art as having ever, in a real sense, affected the course of human affairs.[4]

One can understand the problem this creates for artists who wish to make a difference, or to create some kind of impact. Art itself had long lost its capacity to shock. Leo Steinberg has described the dilemma for

2 Ibid., p.xvi

3 Hans Haacke, quoted in Jack Burnham, *Hans Haacke's Cancelled Show at the Guggenheim*, Artforum, June 1971

4. Greenberg responding to T.J. Clark in Buchloh, Guilbaut and Solkin (eds), *Modernism and Modernity: The Vancouver Conference Papers*, The Press of the Nova Scotia College of Art and Design, 1983, p.191

5 L. Steinberg, 'Some of Hans Haacke's Works considered as Fine Art' in Wallis (ed.), *Hans Haacke: Unfinished Business*, The New Museum, 1986, p.8

Lichtenstein in the early 1960s:

The problem for a hopeful scene-making artist ... was how best to be disagreeable.
What he needed was to find a body of subject matter sufficiently odious to offend
even lovers of art.

And as Lichtenstein himself put it:

It was hard to get a painting that was despicable enough so that no one would
hang it – everybody was hanging everything. It was almost acceptable to hang a
dripping paint rag, everyone was accustomed to this. The one thing everyone
hated was commercial art; apparently they didn't hate that enough either.[5]

So a state of disillusion with art is not new. The reality (if we can call it that)
of art's incapacity to make any difference produces a huge crisis for art and
artists who wish to see themselves as having some effect beyond the world
of art.

But the crisis produced by this problem of social ineffec-
tiveness is met by a move away from art into two main directions, the one
of 'culture' and the one of 'theory' and the link word which holds these
together (art, theory, culture) is 'criticism'. First, 'art criticism', second,
'criticism and theory', and third 'critique of cultural politics'. The shift
between these terms is allowed to take place in order for a particular sector
(that of contemporary art spaces), to imagine for itself a role. As the leaflet
tells us, the role of contemporary art spaces is to 'initiate critical debate, but
it might be not so much in the art they show, but in the kinds of critical practices they allow, that their "cutting edge" can still be maintained.'

This development stakes a claim, not for art, but for criti-
cism and in particular for a 'critique of cultural politics'. It is a retreat from
art, implying an ethical position in relation to aesthetics and points to the
huge difficulty surrounding attempts to insist upon the autonomy of aesthetics and the continuing temptation to reduce aesthetic considerations to
a series of ethical dilemmas. (I'm arguing here, not for aesthetics over ethics
but for a materialist criticism which can acknowledge the specificity of formal considerations; the tendency to move in an ethical direction whenever
the formal is approached produces, not only an inadequate aesthetics, but
also an inadequate politics).

The practice of art criticism has undergone a major transformation in the last fifty years, due to the expansion of international art
markets, the influence of the formalism of Greenbergian criticism, and

the relationship between these two phenomena. Curiously, however, Greenbergian formalism restricts itself to the concern with art objects and does not see itself having a formal structure which is also open to scrutiny in formalist terms.But my concern here is with a particular local development of art reviewing, and this follows a recognisable, international pattern in which a tension between criticism and reviewing exists, a tension which involves assumptions of authority based on the contradiction between what we might call the sensibility of common sense (the gut reaction response) on the one hand and on the other a mandarin sensibility based on the primacy and autonomy of aesthetics (a kind of Kantian *a priori*). The result of this encounter between two responses is a divided subject, unable to reconcile the contradictory demands of the practices of reviewing and criticism each of which coincides with one of the two possible responses. The critic/reviewer must then act in an almost psychotic manner, attempting to destroy, through criticism, the object which is the subject of his critique in order to replace it with himself. It is through this means that self-realisation is possible. This is why certain practices of newspaper reviewing (particularly in the *Sydney Morning Herald*) refer so little to works of art and devote so much space to the disdain or Spenglerian despair of the critic. The production of art does not depend on the existence of a critic but the determination that some, if not all, art is bad requires the presence of an ostensibly objective critic, who takes on the task of judgment. Take this view for example:

Genuine art criticism ... is concerned to separate good from bad .... Criticism is ruthless in its pursuit of the first rate.[6]

The critic in question is attempting to make an argument against what he calls 'the dominant consumerist mentality' which he sees as 'the most powerful enemy of the making of great art.' But within a few paragraphs he manages to slip into the very same consumerism:

I also believe I am doing the art audience a service by pointing out good work by artists of any age and warning them about the bad. There is no fundamental difference between an art critic who warns about bad or inadequate art and a motoring journalist who advises readers that the brakes on a particular car are likely to fail on sharp corners. Bad expensive paintings have ruined many a good home life with their tedious omnipresent ugliness. Far better art is usually available for much less money.[7]

6 D. Bromfield, 'Criticism in a Cold Climate', *Art Monthly*, No.44, October 1991, p.18

7 Ibid.

This kind of schizophrenia can be readily identified as a feature of art-review writing in Australia, where writers spread themselves thinly across the available outlets, slipping uneasily between the styles required of different newspapers or small magazines. Before looking at some problems of this approach, it might be useful to summarise a certain local development in reviewing.

Reviewing as a practice   Although the importance of art critics or reviewers, is acknowledged however there is relatively little published work which has been done on reviewing as a practice.

A short piece on review writing in Melbourne by George Christofakis and Ernest Healy in the *Artworkers' Union National Magazine* in August 1982 saw review writers as mere lackeys of:

a gallery system which at once promotes and regulates what in art will best serve as advertisement and consolidation for a dominating propertied class, and those who identify with the interests of this class.

Since then, the identification of the problem in these terms has become more blurred, although the analysis remains appealing. References to the work of review writers is made in a number of books on Australian art, such as Richard Haese's *Rebels and Precursors.* Gary Catalano's *Years of Hope: Australian Art and Criticism 1959-1968* concerns itself more with the art than the criticism and although the work of prominent reviewers is dealt with, reviewing is not identified as a practice in itself.

Reviewing continues to be regarded as mere caption of art, a position which nobody seriously believes it occupies, given the complaints about the power of critics. A paradoxical situation exists; art reviewers are seen to be all powerful, but the practice of reviewing is never seriously considered except in terms of the personalities of particular critics. Reviewing is simply the personal expression of particular personalities, never as an activity which might be viewed separately from the subjectivity of an individual – although review writing takes place only in the contexts of newspapers in which the constraints of sub-editing and space limitations determine what gets published.

This 'writing as expression' approach is one which reduces the practice of reviewing to one of mere intentionality, an approach which is no longer accepted as being all there is to the production of the objects which the practice of reviewing deals with.

One of the more useful attempts to consider reviewing as a practice is the late Allen Vizents's paper, *Words and Phrase: Reviews by Ted Snell* (*Praxis*, 1985). Vizents's article is based on a relation to language which assumes a notion of objective truth, or rather, a distaste for subjective language in the process of criticism, of a kind represented in the 1950s and 1960s by the *New Criticism*, and deals specifically with the language of review writing in a formal sense.

However, by far the most useful article to seriously address reviewing as a practice – and specifically a practice of writing – is Meaghan Morris's, *In-digestion: A Rhetoric of Reviewing* (*Filmnews*, June 1983). This article is about film criticism/reviewing but the comments wabout the practice of reviewing apply equally to the newspaper reviewing of art.

Morris employs a distinction between reviewing and criticism which goes beyond the usual moral distinction between the two (that is, reviewing is done by Dumb people and Bad writers; criticism is done by Intelligent people and Good writers); Morris, drawing on and extending distinctions made by John Flaus, provides four differences between the two activities (I've reworded these to apply to art):

If all art production ceased tomorrow, criticism would continue but reviewing would not.

Reviewing assumes that the reader hasn't seen the work; criticism assumes that the reader has, will or should have seen the work.

Reviewing is a signifying practice in which pre-existing formal constraints are primary and determining.

A review is a signifying element in the discourse of the medium in which it appears. It is not a parasite on the work of artists nor an extension of a personality, but a bit of a newspaper, a journal, a radio programme, a television show.

The advantage of Morris's approach is that reviewing is taken as a serious activity with a formal structure which can be usefully analysed for the purposes of better understanding the overall industry in which it is situated.

Other attempts have been made to deal with the language of art reviewing in Australia: IMA forum in Brisbane in 1985 (*Art Criticism in Queensland*)[8] and at the Art Association of Australia conference, in Melbourne in mid 1986.[9]

8 Graham Coulter-Smith, *Art Criticism in Queensland*, IMA Brisbane, 1986

9 Benjamin Roger (ed.), *Practices of Criticism in Australia, papers of the AAA*, 1986, vol.1

10 'St Petersburg or Tinsel Town? Melbourne and Sydney: Their differing styles and changing relation', *Meanjin*, 1/1981

11 G. Catalano, *Years of Hope: Australian Art and Criticism 1959-1968*, p.23

Questions of the local   Considerations of Australian art are required to deal with
the inscriptions of different localities on each practice. My
emphasis here is on Sydney critics and the present cultural dominance of
Sydney is cause for much objection from other centres: a one-day seminar
was held by *Meanjin* in Melbourne in 1980 to consider what it regarded as
'the cultural undertow towards Sydney' and to explore the differences
between Melbourne and Sydney.[10]

Among the many factors which have often blunted Sydney's
appreciation of art has been the manner in which the city's newspapers have
presented the subject. John Douglas Pringle, then editor of the *Sydney
Morning Herald*, had more than adequate cause to comment on this in 1958:

*Painting, indeed, has acquired a certain social glamour, and smart women
attend all the openings of exhibitions in order to be photographed by the press
standing in front of pictures which they have not even bothered to look at ... there
is still something deeply wrong in the attitude of even the more intelligent
Australians towards the arts. For them it is always a luxury, a varnish added to
the surface of life and not an essential part of it.*
*Varnish – or on reflection, nail-polish – is the exact term with which to describe
most of the city's institutions devoted to the betterment of the arts.*[11]

Although the question of place exists as a relevant factor in determining
work, the emphasis on place reduces the discussion to a question of different personalities as they are formed in and by different localities; cities,
centres.

My objection to this is not so much it's irrelevant – some of
the most interesting work is currently being done around the question of
place, and more especially, space (issues of resistant regionalism, questions
of post-colonialism, etc.). However, in Australia, the debate turns around a
subjectivism which insists that certain personalities are the main product of
difference at this level, so we end up with very boring debates and personality clashes and a tedious egocentricity in which public spectacles of battle
are engineered every so often between various would-be warriors. I'm
thinking here of the McDonald-Nixon-Parr-Bromfield-Fuller syndrome
in which no-one ever knows the issues which are at stake but the proper
names pass into circulation as ciphers for an absent exchange of ideas. This
has the effect of enhancing (or at times depreciating) the market value of
the work of the protagonists and is a spectacle which seems only to exist in
(and for) the artwork. In other contexts – for example in recent debates

about cultural studies and cultural policy, acknowledgement is made to there being something else is at stake.

In the last fifty years a small number of people have determined what is worthy of consideration in contemporary art in Australia, and a different set of priorities and values probably exists in each city. If we consider the period from the early 1940s to the late 1980s, fewer than ten people have been the principle art reviewers in the *Sydney Morning Herald*. From 1942-57, the position was held by Paul Haefliger, indicating either a considerable deal of power held by the critic, or it perhaps simply that art was not very important and nobody cared who reviewed it. It is very easy to assume that critics wield tremendous power, even though other factors are perhaps more important than the individual critic. Internationally, over this same period, Greenberg was certainly a powerful figure, but this is also the period of US cultural ascendancy, which Greenberg served (rather than caused). It is not until after this period that any real effect of 'international' style was felt in Australia, in spite of advocates for it. Australian art had other concerns and these have been well documented. From 1953 Wallace Thornton wrote for the *Herald* and continued until 1968, with relief provided by Donald Brook in the mid-1960s. Nancy Borlase took over from Thornton and continued until the early 1980s, when Terence Maloon became critic. From the mid-1980s, the position begins to fragment, with a number of critics taking on the role. The expansion of the art market in this period gives the critic an authority which may be undeserved, but another structural factor increases the power which the position is thought to hold: the privileging of the art reviewer in the Saturday review pages. While book reviews occupy much more space in the *Herald* on Saturdays, and numerous writers contribute, the art review has usually been written by a single critic and is a longer, more featured piece of writing than any of the individual book reviews. This structure allows for the emergence of a degree of self-importance and pomposity in the Saturday reviewer, which is intensified by the size of the audience which a daily newspaper critic has. Over this period, the expansion of the small art magazine sector has resulted in a massive increase in writing about art, and although the mainstream media pays attention to this sector from time to time, generally emphasising the incomprehensibility of the language within it, it is the small magazine sector which retains the intellectual authority, a fact which accounts for some of the hostility which more populist media and reviewing practices direct at the sector.

Over this fifty years period, there has been a 100 per cent increase in the number of art reviews in the *Herald*, but more significantly, there has been a much larger increase in the space given to reviews. In 1946, the average review occupied under 10cm^2 of newspaper space. In 1986, this had increased to over 50cm^2 but since then has dropped back somewhat, reflecting perhaps the collapse of the contemporary art market.

A substantial shift took place in the nature and function of review writing over this period, reflected in the choice of critics. Until Terence Maloon succeeded Nancy Borlase as reviewer, the previous reviewers (with the exception of Donald Brook) had been practising artists and writers; since the retirement of Nancy Borlase, the reviewers have all been writers, rather than artists. This is not a practice which is common to all newspapers (*The Australian's* reviewers are also artists a factor which has not been without its controversy).

Whereas the practice of reviewing was once seen to be a non-specialist activity, one which an artist was considered to be the most qualified to perform now, in some contexts at least, reviewing is seen to be a practice of writing. A distinct division of labour has therefore evolved over this period, and is indicative of shifts which have taken place within Australian art in its attempts to situate itself internationally.

This shift has not taken place in Australian art alone, as the reviewing pages of newspapers now indicate, but is a feature of cultural criticism more generally; musicians do not review music; actors and directors do not review films and theatre, etc. This work is done by writers who are specialists in their field or by journalists not necessarily specialists in their field, but primarily writers.

Reviewing is a professional activity in itself, separate from its object of discussion, an autonomous activity seen to have its own structure, language and rules; an activity which can be seen to be a process, productive of the very objects of its analysis. This is not to say that reviewing has become more important than the cultural object to which it refers, but that the relation between the practice of reviewing and the practice of producing an object has changed, has become more complex and it is no longer possible to consider reviewing as being merely parasitic on the object. Rather, the review has become, much more crucially, part of the packaging of the object to which it refers and enters, much more clearly, into its process of production and circulation.

Reviewing has of course always operated in this way; but in

the past, the relation has been denied, a denial made possible by the use of artists as reviewers – as translators, in a sense, of the artist's intentions. This approach assumes the writing of a review is a transparent medium, that the words do not function in their own right, but are mere labels which hang from the work, to be torn off and discarded at will. However, when writers take over the activity of reviewing, the review becomes a work itself, to be considered as writing, a discrete and self-conscious practice, one which cannot deny its own existence, as writing.

By the 1980s a multiplicity of aesthetic styles challenges critics in different ways. The reviewing process itself has changed substantially, and reviewers have had to deal with the spectre of post-modernism and its refusals of the position traditionally occupied by the fine arts; the appropriation of popular culture, the 'quotation' of art historical reference, the anti-aesthetic of a second-generation conceptualism have all rendered the critic's usual resort to standards and authority somewhat irrelevant. However, in the most recent work, we are seeing a return to the supposed certainty of aesthetic values, an insistence on the primacy of the visual as a pre-verbal order of knowledge, coinciding in the first place with the return of the market as prime arbiter of value and then with its collapse. The decline of the art-market and the loss of value which accompanies this involves a search for more permanent values – rather like a 'gold standard' – with self-styled arbiters of tastes (and old-guard positivists) returning to declare the end of modern art again.

Kaucyila Brooke

Are You Politically Correct?

Are You Politically Correct?
is one of a series collected
under the title *Thirteen
Questions* which refers to
a room-mate questionnaire
used by a women's collective
household in which Kaucyila
Brooke lived during the late
1970s. She has also
completed *Are You Neat
or Messy?* and *The Food
Question – Food Habits?
Share Food?* Kaucyila Brooke
co-produced the videotape
Dry Kisses Only with Jane
Cottis. She lives in Los
Angeles and is a member
of the faculty at California
Institute of the Arts.

Entrance to
Leisure World
Laguna Hills,
California

I first heard the expression 'Politically Correct' in 1976
just after I'd moved to the Eugene area. Eugene's
Feminist Community was politically active, educated
and diverse and at the time it centered around a group of
Marxist Feminists who formed the bookstore collective
and were affectionately called the 'Commies'

**Correct? Now that's an odd
idea in a corrupt world**

When I heard some-
one at a general community meeting say that they didn't think
that something or other was 'politically correct', I thought they
were joking. But when I looked
around, I realized that no one was laughing. I began to think that 'The Matriarchy'
might not be the solution after all. ➤

**Abject is
more like it**

**Alienated labour
is still trying to
reunite with its
body at The Family
Fitness Center**

By lesbians, for lesbians and about lesbians?

Ky the time I moved into Hansen Lane, I wasn't quite so green. I decided that working in a shelter for battered women would do more to improve the general conditions for women than involving myself in battles about separatism or the status of male children within the lesbian community. ➢

W

When I found out that women in Seattle argued that penetration in lesbian lovemaking was 'incorrect' because it was too heterosexual, I was upset that women were trying to define each other's desires. ➤

BLACK T-SHIRT

That'd be like taming my wild tongue to only tell one tale

I've been working on a citizen's task force to select new history texts for public schools with multicultural perspectives

We asked interested housemates if they were 'politically correct'. The interviewee would, of course, ask us what we meant by that and that would be the opening for a discussion about personal politics ➤

It's so difficult to find one book for each course that shows the complexities and different contributions of each group

For the time, Elizabeth was basically 'right on', but although she was butch-acting, was learning carpentry, was a vegetarian on a wheatless diet and a volunteer member of the bookstore collective; she did wear the occasional skirt. ➤

SCARF

It's completely ahistorical for the liberal press to call these changes in education 'The New McCarthyism'!

This Star Trek notion of infinite diversity in infinite combination...

Dana was a little more tainted and although she was a working-class lesbian, vegetarian, peace activist, and much sought-after healer; she had a heterosexual married past, a male child from that marriage, and followed a male guru named Baba something or other. ➢

...is perfect for Benneton ads and Coca Cola's 'small world' capitalism.

I was an anarchist-feminist-activist lesbian and I coordinated feminist radio programming. But, I wasn't butch (other lesbians were always sure that I was not a 'real' lesbian), wore skirts and dresses, ate meat occasionally, came from an upper-middle-class WASP family, and I didn't like 'women's music'. ➤

RUSSIAN SAILOR HAT

In political struggle it becomes necessary to suspend commodified individualism into work for common goals

nne was a Jewish Feminist, political songwriter and performer, and she worked with children in preschools introducing them to anti-racist, sexist, classicist and speciesist ideas through music. However, Annie did not define herself as a lesbian and claimed to be polymorphous, had male friends, ate meat and considered the possibility of one day having a male lover. ➤

I've always been uncomfortable with speeches when the audience claps for the ideas it believes in

But these neutralised academic disciplines like 'gender studies' worry me

wisa was a lesbian who worked at a collective hippie restaurant. She liked to watch cable TV and wrote feminist Star Trek fanzines which were sometimes porno-graphic but always heterosexual. ➤

As we moved through these conflicting identities some women were entertained and joined in and others become uncomfortable about the number of differences that existed.

From '13 Questions'

BY KAUCYILA BROOKE

Visual AIDS

Or How to Have Art (Events)

Robert Atkins

Robert Atkins is an art historian, columnist for the *Village Voice*, and co-curator of the touring exhibition *From Media to Metaphor: Art About AIDS*. His most recent book *ArtSpoke: A Guide to Modern Ideas, Movements and Buzzwords, 1848-1944*, is a 'prequel' to his best-seller, *ArtSpeak: A Guide to Contemporary Ideas, Movements and Buzzwords, 1945-present* (1990).

When you reach the answering machine at Visual AIDS's tiny New York office the current message solemnly intones: 'This is Visual AIDS – the creators of *Day Without Art*, *Night Without Light*, and the *Ribbon Project*' During the month preceding *Day Without Art*, this self-promoting little spiel is partly intended to inform journalists of a few simple – and apparently easily-confused – facts: that Visual AIDS is an organisation, that *Day Without Art* is an event, that International AIDS Awareness Day is the World Health Organisation's baby, etc.

Visual AIDS formally appeared in the fall of 1988. It was preceded by perhaps six months of informal and sporadic discussions among four gay, white men: myself, William Olander (the now deceased, New Museum of Contemporary Art curator), Thomas Sokolowski (the director of New York University's Grey Art Gallery) and Gary Garrels (formerly of the DIA Foundation, and now the Walker Art Center). Between us we'd volunteered and buddied at the Gay Men's Health Crisis, raised hell with ACT UP, raised funds for Art Against AIDS, and would continue to do these things after the emergence of Visual AIDS. In our roles as curators and critics, we were also tracking a growing body of artwork about AIDS and trying to give it visibility:

The four of us share a view of the art world as the 'consciousness industry', to borrow the term Hans Haacke borrowed from Hans Magnus Enzensberger. We also shared a belief that artists and arts institutions might play a consciousness-raising role in this crisis. We saw a range of organisations and activities from the exhilarating direct action of ACT UP, to the fund-raising practices of AmFAR

Adapted from an address delivered at the School of the Art Institute of Chicago, 2 December 1992

Visual AIDS can be reached at 131 W. 24th St., New York, NY 10011, tel (212) 206-7658, fax (212) 206-8159

via Art Against AIDS, but we were uninterested in replicating something that already existed. So we looked back to activist art collectives such as the Art Workers' Coalition, which sponsored an art world anti-Vietnam War moratorium in 1969; PADD (Political Art Documentation and Distribution) and Artists Call Against US Intervention in Central America, which organised shows and streetworks that drew attention to the Central American chaos of the early 1980s fermented by the Reagan-Bush regime.

On 1 March 1989, Visual AIDS issued its first press release, signed by 35 multi-cultural representatives of New York artist organisations, museums, and AIDS-service organisations. Entitled *Visual AIDS: The Art World Organises*, the initial, stated goals were modest, but they did lay the foundations for the future. 'Our purpose', we wrote, 'is to support an ongoing effort ... to encourage, facilitate, and highlight AIDS-related exhibitions and programmes in the non-commercial art world .... We hope to increase awareness and encourage discussion of these programmes and the pressing social issues that AIDS raises within American society.' As good art workers we created a slide archive and began to network. That press release ends by noting that: 'an idea involving a moratorium has been proposed to about thirty organisations. [It is] tentatively called *A Day Without Art*.'

Our fledgling organisation was quickly overwhelmed by *Day Without Art*. The event revealed the flimsy, ad hoc nature of our enterprise. We chose not to fund-raise for ourselves in the face of the dire shortage of money for People With AIDS, so at first we operated out of our homes and workplaces. In Fall 1989, office space in the Clocktower was provided by PS1, and later by the generous Art Matters Foundation.

▲ The Guggenheim Museum shrouded in black for the first *Day Without Art* on 1 December 1989

Planning for the first *Day Without Art* proceeded in the most decentralised fashion. We subtitled *Day Without Art* 'a national day of mourning and action in response to the AIDS crisis'. We wanted to encourage – and link – both responses but hoped that the less threatening 'mourning' might allow for the sometimes more controversial 'action'. Our inability to co-ordinate a widely-dispersed national effort initially seemed a weakness, but proved to be an advantage. Local responses became the heart of a so-called national event.

▶ Keith Haring painting his Viral Images murals for the first *Day Without Art* on 1 December 1989, at Pasadena's Art Centre College of Design

The decision of whether or not to participate in *Day Without Art* catalysed dozens of alternately inspirational, acrimonious, and invariably educational discussions among trustees of universities and museums about the roles their institutions might play in battling the AIDS crisis. An astonishing number of generally conservative institutions did decide to participate, many due to pressure from staff members.

More than 800 US arts and AIDS groups participated in the first *Day Without Art*. Some spaces closed for the day, while at others staffers volunteered at AIDS-service organisations. Other organisations and galleries dimmed lights, shrouded – or removed – artwork and replaced it with AIDS-prevention information. Universities and art schools made brilliant use of the day to educate students about AIDS, racism, and homophobia. Children's museums in Boston, Brooklyn, Manhattan, and Pittsburgh provided AIDS programming for kids in the form of plays, videos, poster-making, and discussions. The Iowa Arts Council sponsored an AIDS-awareness poster competition for secondary-school students and exhibited the winners in the state Capital.

With less than six-months' notice, at least 45 spaces mounted exhibitions devoted exclusively to art about AIDS. Video Data Bank's excellent six-hour programme, *Video Against AIDS*, and panels from *The NAMES Project Quilt* were widely exhibited. Until 1989, the Quilt had never been shown in a museum.

For that first *Day Without Art*, solo shows were devoted to AIDS works by Luis Cruz Azaceta, Felix Gonzalez-Torres, Louise Lawler, Hillary Leone and Jennifer MacDonald, Ann Meredith, Brian

Weil, Krysztof Wodiczko, performer Tim Miller, and film-maker Rosa Van Praunheim, to name just a few whose work might be familiar. Keith Haring painted a 24-foot x 10-foot mural depicting 'Viral Images' at the Art Center College of Design in Pasadena during the course of the day. (Keith asked that his mural hang in its present location until a cure is found.) Memorial exhibitions commemorated the artists Philip Dimitri Galas, Richard Irwin, Peter Hujar, Cookie Mueller, Rod Rhodes, Andreas Senser, and Paul Thek. The curators and administrators Nathan Kolodner, John McCarron, Bill Olander, the collector Sam Wagstaff, and the dealer-painter Nicholas Wilder were also celebrated and mourned via exhibition.

It is difficult to summarise hundreds of often inventive observations of the day. At one end of the spectrum were artist organisations that (anonymously) donated both people power and expertise in areas like graphics to AIDS service organisations. At its other end were glitzy observations like the Museum of Modern Art's; MoMA screened *Common Threads* – the HBO-produced film about the NAMES Project Quilt – and Elizabeth Taylor introduced it. The previous night MoMA had staged a vigil and programme highlighted by the premiere of an original composition composed and performed by Leonard Bernstein.

At Visual AIDS, we had only the vaguest sense of what would transpire on 1 December and how it would be received. Perhaps what was surprising was that the element of spectacle was largely absent from the individual observations. Nor did AIDS-as-spectacle dominate the copious and supportive press coverage of the day at a time when AIDS seemed to be slipping, once again, from the media front burner. Interestingly, we found that cultural reporters were much better targets for the AIDS information and rationales for the day than their science- and news-reporter counterparts. Even more interesting, journalists at the major daily papers in Sarasota and Los Angeles wondered why more local organisations were not participating in *Day Without Art*, provoking heated local debate. It's difficult to imagine another situation in which middle-class arts professionals might be forced to defend their decision to remain uninvolved in AIDS struggles.

Visual AIDS's propensity to stimulate debate was first clear a month before *A Day Without Art*. On 8 November 1989, the then-new National Endowment for the Arts Chairman John Frohnmayer inadvertently kicked off *Day Without Art* when he announced that he was rescinding a grant to Artists' Space for Witnesses Against Our Vanishing, the

AIDS exhibition organised by photographer Nan Goldin for *Day Without Art*. Both censorship and AIDS awareness became issues in this tense stand-off between progressive elements of the arts communities and Frohnmayer, who was then busily cosying up to reactionary Senator Jesse Helms.

Because the show was conceived for *Day Without Art*, Visual AIDS found itself well-sited to intervene. After a concerted lobbying effort, Frohnmayer agreed to hold a 1 December meeting organised by Visual AIDS, that would include HIV positive artists. The meeting resulted in the revitalisation of the AIDS Working Group within the federal agency and NEA directives to its organisational mailing lists about compliance with the Disabilities Act and treatment of HIV-positive staff.

▲ Glenn Ligon's
Broadside, one of several
artist-designed,
educational, multi-
purpose images produced
by Visual Aids in 1992

It also spurred some ultimately fruitless work by the NEA regarding health insurance reform.

Because Visual AIDS straddled both the AIDS and art worlds, we began to function as a forum, a meeting place for emerging art-AIDS coalitions. We participated in the NEA's 1991 forum on AIDS and insisted that artists with AIDS be included in the meeting. We hosted the NEA's 1992 meeting of founders and arts professionals that led to the recommendation to implement the second phase of the Estate Project designed to assist artists with AIDS. In 1991, we organised the World AIDS Day Coalition for the World Health Organisation and a spectrum of AIDS organisations, although we ultimately felt that the participants saw us as only as a vehicle for enhanced media attention. And of course we worked with the Coalition United for AIDS Action, which organised the AIDS demonstration and rally during the 1992 Democratic National Convention in New York. Visual AIDS received the New York Governor's Art Award for the first *Day Without Art*.

At the black-tie awards ceremony at the Metropolitan Museum in June 1990, our acceptor, Philip Yenawine, took the opportunity to chide Governor Cuomo for his lackadaisical approach to the AIDS crisis. At that time, we were also feeling organisational growing pains. Our structure had been democratic-anarchic: we had a steering committee and a meeting chairperson but no officers. Now we were being offered foundation money

The second *Day Without Art* approached and overwhelmed us as thoroughly as the first had. Our organisational circle had grown so large that producing more than a couple of mailings each year had become prohibitively costly. In 1990, we urged participating organisations to get beyond the 'art ghettos' and out into the community – that is, communities. Urging was about all we've ever been able to do and it's hard to know what effect that urging had.

Day Without Art 1990 signified a radical shift within the group. Our artist population increased substantially. This made us a livelier, more spirited bunch, but it sometimes gave us less access to useful contacts and our organisation constituents. Ideas remained our currency and in 1990 we began producing them at a rapid clip. The boundaries between programmes and programmatic artwork began to blur. We operated like an art collective, which I found extremely satisfying. A half-dozen new projects sprang up like mushrooms. *Positive Actions: the Visual AIDS Competition* was a competition for a temporary public artwork about AIDS to be funded by the Public Art Fund. Entrants were asked to consider these questions: Can art and design make a difference as friends and colleagues confront HIV infection? What can we do as artists and citizens in the public arena to inform, move, inspire, and/or provoke audiences? What sort of physical, social, or political sites would be appropriate for a work about AIDS?

The 'Editors' Project' was a way of coercing the normally not very receptive art magazines to do more about AIDS. Ranging from *After Image* to *Artforum*, and from *Contemporanea* to *Shift*, eleven of them published different fragments of Group Material's AIDS Timeline in their December issues. 'Night Without Light' saw the skylines of New York and San Francisco darkened for fifteen minutes and this symbolic observance was repeated throughout the US in 1991 and 1992.

Another project that debuted on 1 December 1990, was the *Electric Blanket*, an outdoor slide-projection event. Information and statistics about AIDS and photo-images of PWAs were projected onto the side of the Cooper Union in the East Village while bands played. Most of the pictures had been gathered in the neighbourhood, making this a very local tribute. The *Electric Blanket* has been exhibited inside or outside art spaces from Seattle to Hamburg. It continues to travel and is augmented as often as possible with local images. Perhaps the 1990 project with the most audience-potential was Bravo cable network's *Moment Without Television*, followed by 48-hours of continuous AIDS programming. Bravo's ground-breaking work continues for its third year and has apparently inspired PBS and MTV to wake up and follow suit. Visual AIDS has initiated other artists' programmes, but I know you get the idea. I want to turn to just one other Visual AIDS-instigated project that's not specifically connected with *Day Without Art*. I want to discuss it because it's quite misunderstood and it's underestimated. Its slyly subversive character is also emblematic of the way Visual AIDS has operated. That project is *The Ribbon Project* – which is the way our trademark reads – but you know it as *The Red Ribbon*.

Wear a red ribbon to show your commitment to the fight against AIDS. The red ribbon demonstrates compassion for people with AIDS and their caretakers; and support for education and research leading to effective treatments, vaccines, or a cure.

Self Taught/Self Represented
Homeless Women and AIDS

▲ Artists Juli Carson and Aaron Keppel helped women in a New York homeless shelter produce this Aids awareness poster. The project was conceived and co-ordinated by the Artist and Homeless Collaborative with assistance from Visual Aids

The red ribbon debuted on the televised Tony Award Ceremonies in late Spring 1991, and now you can't turn on the television without seeing them. We knew how subversive the ribbon was, when – a full fifteen months after its creation – Republican handlers ripped it off Barbara Bush's chest at the 1992 Republican convention in Houston.

The ribbon has enabled writers who do think and talk about AIDS to write about it. *New York Newsday* ran an article titled 'Red Ribbon to AIDS Kindness' on 6 October 1992, about the apparently red ribbon-strewn Miss America pageant. Bear in mind that the ribbon is hardly news any more. In fact, one might assume that the ribbon is simply mandatory accessorising at any television event or one might alternately assume that it continues to symbolise AIDS-concern, or both. Certainly people wear red ribbons for the 'wrong' reasons, just as people wore silence=death buttons for a variety of reasons (occasionally in order to get laid). All the same, I am absolutely convinced that the red ribbon never deterred anybody from doing something more meaningful to end the AIDS crisis.

In any case, I did learn from the 'Red Ribbon to AIDS Kindness' article that the new Miss America volunteers in an AIDS hospice, doesn't believe that the Bush-Quayles have done enough to combat the epidemic, and plans to continue to talk publicly about AIDS during her reign. The author ended his column with a stirring denunciation of AIDS-phobia and homophobia. It's unclear to me whether Miss America's or the writer's comments would have appeared before the advent – or should I say onslaught? – of the ribbon.

If I've given you the impression that Visual AIDS is largely the sum of its project parts, that's probably not inaccurate. This organisational umbrella-of-a-structure has made it easier to respond to quick changing AIDS realities. Certainly the one thing we have learned from AIDS-work is that AIDS crises are dynamic. What was needed or useful yesterday, is irrelevant or *passé* today. The *ad hoc* nature of the group has also allowed for a fluid membership where satisfaction derives from working on a project, rather than simply belonging to an organisation in which 'membership' is, frankly, a bit of a *non-sequitur*. Visual AIDS faces what every AIDS organisation faces: Burn-out and the illness of many of our most active members. We also face changes in the art world – some of them positive. Over the past four years there's been an attitudinal sea-change in the acceptance of tough, AIDS-related content in exhibited artwork. Such works remind us that art's traditional purpose is to teach. And that the anti-didacticism of so much late modernist art is really an anomaly, an exception in Western art's several thousand-years'-long history. Effective, socially-engaged art practices can help save lives. But only if large and vocal elements within the arts communities help ensure their broadest possible reach.

▼ The Ribbon Project: the red ribbon and the 'official' text that accompanies it

· WEAR A RED RIBBON ·
FOR A CURE

THE RIBBON PROJECT

Wear a red ribbon to show your commitment to the fight against AIDS. The red ribbon demonstrates compassion for people with AIDS and their caretakers; and support for education and research leading to effective treatments, vaccines, or a cure.

The proliferation of red ribbons unifies the many voices seeking a meaningful response to the AIDS epidemic. It is a symbol of hope: the hope that one day soon the AIDS epidemic will be over, that the sick will be healed, that the stress upon our society will be relieved. It serves as a constant reminder of the many people suffering as a result of this disease, and of the many people working toward a cure—a day without AIDS.

The Ribbon Project is a grass roots effort. It is easy to make your own ribbons. Cut red ribbon in 6" length, then fold at the top into an inverted "V" shape. Use a safety pin to attach to clothing.

The Ribbon Project
Visual AIDS Artists' Caucus
131 West 24 Street 3rd floor
New York, NY 10011
tel 212/206-6758 fax 212/206-8159

▲ *The Electric Blanket*, a slide
show of images of PWAs
produced and conceived by the
Visual Aids Artists', Caucus, is
projected on the Cooper Union on
1 December 1990. Photo by Dona
Ann McAdams